Collins

Edexcel GCSE (9–1)
Statistics

Practice Book

T0371159

Rob Ellis

Collins

William Collins' dream of knowledge for all began with the publication of his first book in 1819. A self-educated mill worker, he not only enriched millions of lives, but also founded a flourishing publishing house. Today, staying true to this spirit, Collins books are packed with inspiration, innovation and practical expertise. They place you at the centre of a world of possibility and give you exactly what you need to explore it.

Collins. Freedom to teach.

Published by Collins
An imprint of HarperCollins*Publishers*
The News Building
1 London Bridge Street
London
SE1 9GF

Browse the complete Collins catalogue at
www.collins.co.uk

HarperCollins*Publishers*
Macken House, 39/40 Mayor Street Upper
Dublin 1, D01 C9W8, Ireland

© HarperCollins*Publishers* Limited 2019

10

ISBN 978-0-00-835971-3

All rights reserved. No part of this publication may be reproduced, stored in a retrieval system, or transmitted in any form by any means, electronic, mechanical, photocopying, recording or otherwise, without the prior written permission of the Publisher or a licence permitting restricted copying in the United Kingdom issued by the Copyright Licensing Agency Ltd, Barnard's Inn, 86 Fetter Lane, London, EC4A 1EN.

British Library Cataloguing-in-Publication Data
A catalogue record for this publication is available from the British Library.

Author: Rob Ellis
First edition authors: Greg Byrd, Fiona Mapp, Claire Powis and Bob Wordsworth
Publisher: Katie Sergeant
Product manager: Alex Marson
Copyeditor: Julie Bond
Answer checker: Paul Hunt
Proofreader: David Hemsley
Illustrator: Ann Paganuzzi
Cover designer: The Big Mountain
Cover photograph: Shutterstock
Typesetter: Jouve India Private Limited
Production controller: Katharine Willard
Printed and bound in the UK by Ashford Colour Press Ltd

The publishers gratefully acknowledge the permission granted to reproduce the copyright material in this book. Every effort has been made to trace copyright holders and to obtain their permission for the use of copyright material. The publishers will gladly receive any information enabling them to rectify any error or omission at the first opportunity.

MIX
Paper | Supporting responsible forestry
FSC™ C007454

This book contains FSC™ certified paper and other controlled sources to ensure responsible forest management.

For more information visit: www.harpercollins.co.uk/green

Contents

Specification references are shown in brackets after the topic name, e.g. (1b.01-04).

Introduction

Welcome to *Collins Edexcel GCSE (9-1) Statistics Practice Book*. This book is packed full of graded practice questions, ideal for extra homework practice and exam revision.

Question grades

The grade is indicated for every question, with the questions in each exercise gradually increasing in difficulty.

Quick reminders

Remember the key points of a topic with helpful **Quick reminder** sections at the start of each exercise.

Exam practice

Prepare for the GCSE Statistics exam with examination-style questions throughout the book. These questions are labelled **EQ**.

Assessment Objectives

Practise using all of your statistical skills with questions that assess whether you can interpret statistical information and results in context and draw suitable conclusions (**AO2**), and questions that test if you can assess the appropriateness of statistical methodologies and conclusions drawn (**AO3**). All questions targeting these Assessment Objectives are clearly labelled.

There are also plenty of questions that test your knowledge, understanding and application of standard statistical techniques (**AO1**).

Answers

You will find answers to all the questions at the back of the book. If you are working on your own you can check your answers yourself. If you are working in class your teacher may want to go through the answers with you.

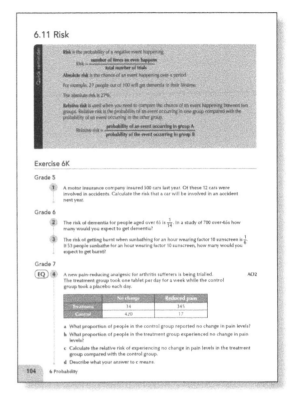

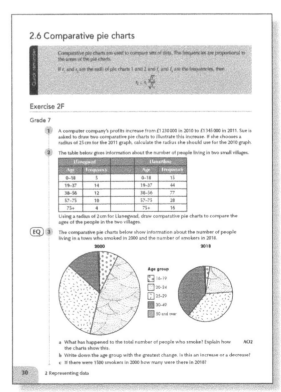

1 Collecting data

1.1 Types of data

Quick reminder

Primary data is data that has been collected by the person who is going to use it.

Secondary data is data that has not been collected by the person who is going to use it, e.g. from published databases.

Raw data is data that has been collected but has not been sorted or processed in any way.

Data is either **qualitative** or **quantitative**.

Qualitative data describes the quality of a variable and is not numerical, e.g. yes/no answers, colour, type of pet.

Quantitative data is numerical, e.g. number of pets, distance travelled to work.

Quantitative data can be either **discrete** or **continuous**.

Discrete data is data that can be counted and can only take particular values, e.g. number of pets, shoe size.

Continuous data is data that can be measured, and can take any value on a scale, e.g. distance to work, height, time taken to complete a task.

When you want to explore links between two **variables** (e.g. height and weight), data is collected in pairs for the two variables. This is called **bivariate data**.

Exercise 1A

Grade 2

1 Sophie wants to find out about local weather by looking at newspaper reports for the last year. Is this primary or secondary data?

2 Anil wants to find out what his classmates' favourite football teams are. Is this variable qualitative or quantitative?

3 Sharna wants to measure the heights of 50 people. Is this variable discrete or continuous?

EQ 4 A shop sells pencil cases.

Use the best word from the list to complete the sentences below.

  sample   qualitative   discrete   continuous   bias

a The number of pencil cases sold by the shop is _____data.

b The colour of a pencil case is _____data.

c The weight of a pencil case is _____data.

d Ben says that the cost of a pencil case is quantitative data. Explain why Ben is correct.

Grade 3

5 Are these discrete or continuous data?

a The weight of a cat.

b The number of sweets in a bag.

c Shoe size.

d The time it takes to boil an egg.

 6 A doctor's surgery wants to explore its efficiency.

State whether each of the following variables is qualitative, discrete or continuous.

a The number of patients seen each day.

b The time each patient waits to be seen.

c The surgery manager is going to take a random sample of patients to monitor their waiting times. Define random.

Grade 4

7 Rachel is conducting research on trees in her local wood.

a Copy and complete the table below to describe the sort of data she could collect.

Use the words: qualitative, quantitative, discrete and continuous.

Data	Type of data
Species of trees	
Number of trees	
Height of trees	
Circumference of tree trunks	
Number of branches	

b Which two of the data items above could be used as bivariate data?

8 Give two advantages and two disadvantages of collecting primary data.   AO3

 9 A ski resort owner wants to give his guests information about the number of centimetres of snowfall they can expect in January.

a Write down one way he can collect the information if he wants to use primary data.

b Write down one way he can collect the information if he wants to use secondary data.

c Is the data he collects qualitative or quantitative? Explain your answer.

10 Sales staff in a second-hand car showroom have collected information about:

a the most common colours of cars sold in July

b prices of cars sold in July 2018

c number of cars sold in July 2019, compared with July 2018

d makes of cars sold in July

e the average time taken for a member of the sales team to make a sale.

Choose from the terms 'qualitative', 'quantitative', 'discrete' and 'continuous' to describe fully the data in **a**, **b**, **c**, **d** and **e**. More than one term may apply.

EQ **11** Poppy thinks that a person's favourite hobby depends on their age. She plans to use quantitative and qualitative variables to investigate this.

　　a i Write down a quantitative variable that she needs to use in her investigation.

　　　ii Write down a qualitative variable that she needs to use in her investigation.

　　b What is collecting information from every member of a population known as?

　　c Give one advantage of collecting information from every member of　　AO3
　　　the population.

1.2 Petersen capture–recapture formula

Quick reminder

The Petersen capture–recapture formula is used to estimate the size of a population. This is often used to estimate populations of animals or insects. It is done by capturing a sample, marking or tagging them and recapturing a new sample.

The Petersen capture–recapture formula is $N = \dfrac{Mn}{m}$, where:

N = the population estimate

M = the number of animals captured, marked/tagged and released in the first sample

n = the number of animals captured in the second sample

m = the number of marked/tagged animals captured in the second sample.

Exercise 1B

Grade 6

1 A naturalist wants to know how many kittiwakes there are in a bird colony. He captures 55, tags them, and then releases them. Seven days later he captures 100 kittiwakes and finds that 12 of them are tagged. Estimate how many kittiwakes are in the colony.

2 Bethan is tracking the decline in humpback whales. It was estimated that in 1966 there was a population of 120 000. Between 2016 and 2018 Bethan tags 600 whales. Over the next year Bethan observes 120 whales and finds that two of them are tagged.

　　a Estimate the current population.

　　b By what percentage has the whale population declined?　　AO2

3 A manager of a children's indoor play centre wants to estimate the number of balls in the ball pit. She does not want to count them all, so she marks 100 and mixes them back in. She then picks 150 out of the pit at random and finds that two have been marked.

　　a Calculate an estimate of the number of balls in the pit.

　　b Why does she not need to pick out the first 150 balls at random?　　AO3

4 Kate runs a 'guess the number of sweets in the jar' competition at a summer fete. **AO2**
The following guesses are made:

   Dave – 210, Tom – 312, Rob – 412, Chris – 521, Non – 113, Emily – 634, Humza – 297

She takes 30 sweets and replaces them with identically sized wooden beads. She puts them back into the jar and mixes them in thoroughly. She then removes another 20 sweets out of the jar and finds that three of them are wooden beads. Who won the competition?

5 A beekeeper wants to estimate the number of bees in a hive. He captures 200 and marks them. Two months later he captures another 200 and finds that two are marked.

a Estimate the number of bees in the hive.

b Why might this not be an accurate estimate? **AO3**

EQ **6** A gamekeeper wants to estimate the number of fish in a lake on an estate. He catches a sample of 40 fish from the lake. He marks each fish and then carefully returns them to the lake. The next day the gamekeeper catches 20 fish from the lake. He finds that five of them are marked.

a Estimate the total number of fish in the lake.

b Write down any assumptions you made. **AO3**

1.3 Census data

Quick reminder

What's the difference between a census and a survey?

A census collects data from everyone or everything in a population, whereas a survey collects data from a sample of the population as a whole.

	Advantages	Disadvantages
Census	Takes the whole population into account Accurate data Unbiased (as all asked)	Expensive Time consuming Can be difficult to make sure you have responses from the whole population Large quantity of data produced
Survey	Cheaper Less time consuming A more manageable amount of data produced	Not completely representative of whole population Sampling method may inadvertently introduce bias

Exercise 1C

Grade 3

 1 An estate agent wants to get information about house prices in the town where he works.

a What population should he use? Give a reason for your answer.

b Why might he not want to use a census of the house prices? **AO3**

2 A town council wants to know what people think about the plan to build a new shopping centre.

It decides to take an opinion poll of residents' views.

a Give one reason why the council should not take a census. **AO3**

b From what population should it take a sample. Give a reason for your answer.

Grade 4

3 A market research company is going to conduct a national opinion poll. **AO3**

They want to find out what people think about current licensing laws (the times that pubs and clubs can open and close).

Give **two** reasons why it would not be a good idea to carry out a census.

4 A market research company wants to find out customers' views about a new **AO3** mobile phone shop that has just opened.

Should they take a census or survey a sample of their customers?

Give a reason for your answer.

5 The manager of a factory wants to carry out a survey to find out the workers' **AO3** views on the menu in the factory canteen.

Should the manager take a sample survey or a census?

Give **two** reasons for your answer.

Grade 5

 6 A city council is trying to decide where it should build a new school. **AO3**

Should they take a sample survey or a census?

Give a reason for your answer.

1.4 Sampling

When data is being collected, you will need to take a **sample** of the population being investigated. A **sample frame** is used to identify the population. To avoid **bias**, the size of the sample and the method by which it is selected need to be carefully considered.

Name	Method
(Simple) random sample	Each member of the population is numbered. A random number table or a random number generator on a calculator/computer is used to select members for the sample.
Stratified sample	The population is divided into groups (strata). The same proportion of each group is identified to make up the sample so that the sample mirrors the population as a whole. Members are then selected within each group using a random process.
Systematic sample	A starting point is chosen at random. The data items are then chosen at regular intervals from this point (e.g. every fifth person on a list) depending on the size of the sample required.
Quota sample	A number (quota) of identified groups is interviewed, e.g. 20 men age 20–24 …
Cluster sample	The population can be put into or falls naturally into groups or clusters. A sample of groups is chosen randomly and each member of these groups is included.
Judgement sample	The sample is selected using the judgement of the researcher.
Opportunity sample (convenience sample)	This sample is selected using who or what is available at a sample location, i.e. asking a sample of people in a city centre their views.

Exercise 1D

Grade 3

 1   Write the name of the sampling method that is being used in the examples below.

 a Andrew needs a sample of 20 people from a numbered list of 100. He generates 20 random numbers and uses those numbered people.

 b Emma wants to select a sample of 10 of her classmates. She uses a random number to identify her first person, then takes every third person on the class register until she has her sample.

 c A supermarket manager requires a sample of 20 from her workforce of 60 women and 40 men. She randomly selects 12 women and 8 men.

2 A researcher wants to find out shoppers' opinions of a newly designed town shopping centre. She asks the first 20 people entering a coffee shop.

  a What type of sampling is this?

  b Describe one advantage and one disadvantage of this type of sampling. AO3

3 A market researcher wants to find out people' views on a newly formed political party. He selects 10 people to interview outside a supermarket.

  a What type of sampling is this?

  b Give one advantage and one disadvantage of this type of sampling. AO3

Grade 4

4 Here is an extract from a table of random numbers.

```
48  59  32    38  11  85    84  93  02    29  34  80    94  03  28    57  39  49
52  40  23    21  03  32    72  94  49    49  32  92    02  74  92    24  05  31
47  72  07    94  02  75    69  45  22    84  92  03    39  58  20    05  83  82
82  11  84    74  93  38    37  42  90    31  39  28    59  20  52    43  39  27
```

  a Select 10 random numbers each less than 50. Start at the top left-hand corner and work across in pairs from left to right.

  b Select 10 random numbers each less than 50. Start at the top left-hand corner and work down in pairs, and from left to right.

EQ 5 A teacher wants to undertake a survey about the number of hours of television AO3
that students watch in a week. He considers three possible methods for the survey:

Method 1: Give the survey to the first 40 students seen in a week.

Method 2: Choose 40 students at random.

Method 3: Choose 26 students, picking one whose surname begins with each letter of the alphabet.

  a Give a reason why Method 3 is not suitable.

  b Which of the other two methods for doing the survey will give the most reliable results?

  Give a reason for your choice.

Grade 5

6 A primary school has three age groups. The first age group has 60 children, the second has 40 children and the third has 20 children.

Describe how you would get a sample of 30 children, stratified by age.

7 For each of the following situations: AO3

  i identify the population

  ii explain why the sample may be biased

  iii explain a better method to use to choose a sample.

  a Jamilla thinks that girls at her school get more pocket money than boys. There are 300 children at the school: 120 boys and 180 girls. In her survey she asks 30 boys and 30 girls.

  b Kevin wants to find out how far, on average, people in his town travel to work. He asks all the people at his local railway station on a Tuesday morning.

  c To find out attitudes on smoking, an interviewer stopped people in a local shopping centre one weekday morning to ask their views.

8 A local fish and chip shop attempted to estimate the number of people in a certain town who eat fish and chips. One evening they phoned 100 people in the town and asked 'have you eaten fish and chips in the last month?' Forty-seven people said 'yes'. The fish and chip shop concluded that 47% of the town's population eat fish and chips. **AO3**

Give three criticisms of this method of estimation.

Grade 6

9 A university wants to investigate the use of its canteen. It wants to ask a sample of 50 students in total from three year groups.

Year group	Male	Female
1	600	660
2	420	480
3	480	360

It decides to use a stratified sample.

a Describe the strata it will use.

b Work out the number of males and females in each stratum that will be used.

c Describe how it should choose the individual members of the strata.

10 Henry decides to estimate the number of daisies in the grass on the school playing field. He stands on the playing field and counts the number of daisies within 1 metre of his feet.

a What is the population?

b Why may the sample be biased? **AO3**

c Describe a better sampling method that he could use.

11 A machine producing corkscrews is believed to produce defective corkscrews at a rate of 10%. The foreman wants to undertake a systematic sample to test this.

a Why might this not be the best method of sampling? **AO3**

b What would be a better method?

Grade 7

12 The table shows the bookings at a hotel for one month.

Family	Couple	Single Person
93	75	32

The hotel manager wants to send questionnaires to a stratified sample of 30 of these bookings.

Calculate the number of each type of bookings he should include.

13 The table shows the number of people who use the facilities at a local leisure centre on a particular day.

	Male	Female
Swimming pool	106	15
Gym	180	53
Yoga class	6	24
Spin class	6	10

The leisure centre manager wants to undertake a survey to find the reaction of customers to proposed new opening times.

He decides to take a systematic survey of 20 male gym users.

a Explain how this sample could be collected.

b Give **two** reasons why this sample would be unrepresentative of the   **AO3**
customers as a whole.

c As an alternative, the manager is advised to take a sample, stratified by gender and leisure centre use, of 50 of the 400 customers.

   i Calculate the number of customers at the spin class to be included in the sample.

   ii Calculate the number of female yoga class members to be included in the sample.

14

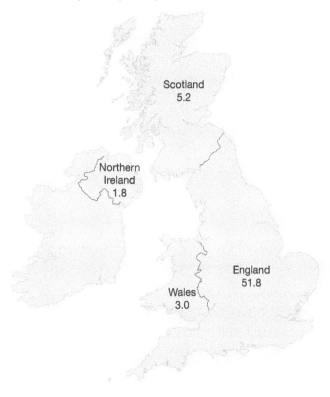

2010 UK Population (millions)

Scotland 5.2

Northern Ireland 1.8

England 51.8

Wales 3.0

a What was the total population of the UK in 2010?

b Calculate how many people from each country would be in a random stratified sample of 500 000.

1.5 Obtaining data

Once you have decided which area you are going to research, you need to decide what data you are going to collect and how you are going to collect it.

You can use secondary data, e.g. from a database or census, or there are various ways that you can collect primary data:

Experiment

In an experiment, at least one of the variables is controlled – the **independent/explanatory variable**. The effect observed is the **dependent/response variable**.

Types of experiment

Laboratory experiments are conducted in a closely monitored environment.

Field experiments are conducted in the test sample's environment. The independent variable can be manipulated.

Natural experiments are conducted in the test sample's environment. Changes in the independent variable are not manipulated, which makes the experiment difficult to repeat.

Surveys

Surveys can be done in a variety of ways including through observation, interviews or questionnaires.

Data collection sheets are used when making observations. They help to make collecting the data easier and organise the data as it is collected.

Questionnaires are a series of questions that are used to gather data. They ensure that everyone is asked the same questions and that the data is collected in an organised way.

Questions need to be clear, not have any **bias** or express opinions.

Tick boxes can be useful in gathering responses, but in setting these up you need to make sure that there are no gaps and no overlaps.

Data logging is a mechanical process for collecting data, such as using a rainfall gauge or counting the number of people that pass through a turnstile.

Cleaning data is a technique that involves removing inaccurate data and extreme values known as outliers.

Exercise 1E

Grade 3

1 Helen wants to find out the number of children in families of pupils in her class. Design a data collection sheet for this data.

2 Ella is going to spin a coin 100 times and record the result. The coin can land on Heads or Tails.

   Design a suitable data collection sheet for Ella.

(EQ) 3 Jez wants to find out the favourite flavour of crisps in his class.

   He asks members of his class to name their favourite flavour and starts to write down their choices in a list: plain, salt and vinegar, plain, etc.

   a Explain why this is not the most efficient way of recording the data.   AO3

   b Design a data collection sheet he could use.

Grade 4

4 Here is a data collection sheet to be used for a survey about the cost of mobile phones.

Give two criticisms of the data collection sheet.

Cost (£)	iPhone	Samsung	Huawei	Sony
0–£25				
£25–£50				
£55–£100				
£105–£150				

5 Alex wants to find out if right-handed people have faster reaction times than left-handed people.

Is the reaction time he measures the dependent variable or the independent variable?

6 A gym wants to find out when most people use it. Explain how a data logging machine could be used.

7 The data collected below is in response to the question: How much pocket money do you get each week?

10.2   £150   90p   £6.00   250   £8.20   450   650p   12.5

Clean and rewrite this data.

8 The heights of 10 males were measured. The results are listed below.

1.54   162 cm   19.2   171   .172   1670   1.82 m   180 cm   158   16.3

Clean and rewrite the data.

Grade 5

9 A newspaper suggests that the older you are, the more likely you are to watch the news on TV. How would you collect data to investigate this hypothesis?

10 A publishing company is given a contract to design and market a lifestyle magazine for exercise enthusiasts.

a Explain how they could use both primary and secondary data.

b Explain a possible method of collecting primary data.

11 Maggie thinks that girls are better at spelling than boys. How could she design an experiment to test this.

EQ **12** Abbi wants to investigate the most popular type and memory capacity of personal computer.

a She could use primary or secondary data. How could she get each type of data?

b Give **two** advantages and **two** disadvantages of using secondary data.   AO3

c Design a data collection sheet that Abbi could use to collect primary data.

1.6 Surveys, questionnaires and interviews

Data for an investigation is often collected by completing a **survey**. This can be done either through **observation**, a **questionnaire** or an **interview**. Choosing the correct method for the investigation is essential.

A **pilot survey** (trial) is often completed to check that the questions are correct and will give the required information before the main survey is undertaken. Questions need to be clear with no **bias**.

Survey type	Advantages	Disadvantages
Observation	Easy to collect data Potentially large amount of data can be collected	Limited data can be collected No follow up Lack of detail Observer may need to be trained – cost
Questionnaire	Low cost Large numbers of participants Easy analysis Can be done online	Low response rate from mail surveys Lack of detail
Interview	Personal contact Ability to probe and ask follow-up questions Detailed answers	Time consuming High cost, including training the interviewer People don't like unsolicited telephone interviews

Definitions

A **respondent** is someone who takes part in a survey.

A **pilot survey** is conducted on a small sample to test the design and methods of the survey.

A **questionnaire** is a set of questions designed to obtain data.

An **open question** is one that has no suggested answers.

A **closed question** has a set of answers for the respondent to choose from. This may be through, for example, tick boxes or a sliding scale.

Extraneous variables are variables that you are not studying in your test, that may affect the outcome.

A **control group** is the group in a study that does not receive treatment and is then used as a benchmark to measure how the other tested subjects do.

Matched pairs is an experimental design where pairs of participants are matched in a variable, such as age, gender, height, IQ etc. One member of each pair is then randomly assigned into the experimental group and the other into the control group.

Exercise 1F

Grade 2

1   A council included this question in a questionnaire:

'Do you agree that the new one way system is a good idea?'

Give one criticism of this question.

Grade 3

2 Edward is carrying out a survey about rugby teams. This is one question from his survey.

> How often do you watch a rugby match?
> ☐ Less than once a week   ☐ Once a week   ☐ Whenever I can

a Give a reason why this is not a good question.

b Rewrite the question to make it a good question.

(EQ) 3 Krishan receives a questionnaire in the post about a new local leisure centre.

Three of the questions are shown below. Give **one** criticism of each question.

Question 1:

How often have you exercised in the last 6 months?

Question 2:

How much do you earn each year? Please tick one box.

☐ Less than £10 000   ☐ £10 000 up to £20 000   ☐ More than £20 000

Question 3:

a If you have already used our leisure centre, give one reason why you enjoyed using it.

b Krishan wants to know how often people visit the new leisure centre. Suggest a suitable question that he could ask.

Grade 4

4 Give **two** advantages and **two** disadvantages of using an interview to gather data.

Grade 5

5 Anita is studying whether drinking beetroot juice improves athletic performance. Participants will run 1000 m without drinking beetroot juice and the following day repeat the test after drinking beetroot juice.

a What is the explanatory variable?   **c** Identify two extraneous variables.

b What is the response variable?

(EQ) 6 Max wants to open a shop in the village where he lives.

To find out the views of local people, he delivers a questionnaire to every house in the village.

a The questionnaire includes a closed question about the respondent's age.

  i Explain what is mean by a *closed question*.

  ii Give one advantage of using a closed question for age.

b Only 14% of the questionnaires are returned to Max.

  Suggest how Max might have improved the response rate.

c The returned questionnaires showed that some of his questions had been badly worded.

Suggest what Max should have done before he delivered his questionnaire to avoid this problem.

d One of Max's questions was:

'How often do you go shopping?'

Give **two** criticisms of this question.

Grade 6

7 A large sports company with 170 shops wants to obtain information about sales. **AO3**

They decide to send out a questionnaire to all shops, but first carry out a pilot survey.

What are the advantages of conducting a pilot survey?

8 You need to carry out a survey to find out how much money people will spend   **AO3**
on a holiday.

a Give one reason why you might choose to carry out a personal interview rather than a postal survey.

b Give one reason why you might not choose to conduct a personal survey.

c Give one advantage and one disadvantage of conducting an online survey about holidays.

Grade 7

9 A researcher wants to test the claim that a slimming tablet can achieve   **AO3**
significant weight loss in a month.

He decides to test this claim on 40 individuals.

He sets up an experimental and a control group using matched pairs.

a Why does he use a control group?   c Identify two extraneous variables.

b How would he select his matched pairs?

1.7 Hypotheses

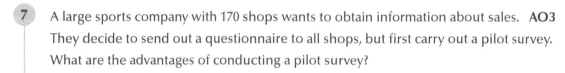

Quick reminder

When you are planning your investigation, it is very important to think carefully about your hypothesis. You must decide what data you will need to test the hypothesis and how you will collect the data. You should also think about what problems you might encounter collecting the data.

As part of your plan, you must think about how you are going to use your data.

Exercise 1G

Grade 5

1 Ying thinks that it is cheaper to buy CDs on the Internet than in high street stores. **AO2**
  a State a hypothesis she could use.
  b What data might she collect?
  c What other factors should she consider?
  d What problems might she have collecting the data?
  e How will she use the data?

2 Florence thinks that a person's memory gets worse as they get older. **AO2**
  a State a hypothesis she could use.
  b What data might she collect?
  c What other factors should she consider?
  d What problems might she have collecting the data?
  e How will she use the data?

3 Daniel thinks boys do better at GCSE Maths than girls. **AO2**
  a State a hypothesis he could use.
  b What data might he collect?
  c What other factors should he consider?
  d What problems might he have collecting the data?
  e How will he use the data?

4 Sam's father thinks that broadsheet newspapers such as *The Times* use longer **AO2**
  words than tabloid newspapers such as *The Sun*. Sam is going to investigate this.
  a State a hypothesis he could use.
  b What data might he collect?
  c What other factors should he consider?
  d What problems might he have collecting the data?
  e How will he use the data?

5 Pritesh thinks boys spend more time playing computer games after school **AO2**
  than girls do.
  a State a hypothesis she could use.
  b What data might she collect?
  c What other factors should she consider?
  d What problems might she have collecting the data?
  e How should she use the data?

6 Hamish wants to check his hypothesis: **AO2**

  'Girls spend less time playing sport than boys do.'

  Explain how Hamish should investigate.

2 Representing data

2.1 Tally charts and frequency tables

Quick reminder

When data is collected it needs to be organised so that it is easy to read. A frequency table has three columns, one for listing the items which have been collected, one for the tally marks, and one to record the frequency of each item. Tally marks are grouped in fives.

Sport	Tally	Frequency
Football	IIII IIII IIII IIII IIII	25
Rugby	IIII IIII IIII III	18
Tennis	IIII IIII II	12
Basketball	IIII IIII IIII IIII II	22

Exercise 2A

Grade 1

1 Members of a class were asked how many pets they had. These are their answers:

1	2	1	2	2	3
6	5	1	5	2	2
1	4	1	4	2	2
2	4	1	3	1	3
3	3	2	3	2	4

a Draw a frequency table to show this information.

b What was the most common number of pets?

c What was the total number of pets?

d How many students had fewer than three pets?

2 Members of a class are asked how many brothers they have. These are their answers:

0	1	1	2	1
1	3	2	2	1
0	1	1	0	1
0	0	1	0	1

a Draw a frequency table to show this information.

b How many students had three brothers?

c How many students had less than two brothers?

3 Esme asked the other children in her class how many pets they had. The responses are listed below:　　　　　　　　　　　　　　　　AO2

    2, 4, 0, 0, 0, 3, 4, 2, 1, 3, 0, 1, 0, 2, 0, 2, 3, 1, 2, 2, 4, 3, 2, 0, 0, 1, 0

a Design and complete a tally chart to present this information. Include a frequency column.

b How many children had no pets?

c How many children did Esme ask?

2.2 Grouped frequency tables

When the data to be collected has a wide range of values, with few values likely to be the same, the data is sorted into groups or classes. These are called **class intervals**.

Exercise 2B

Grade 2

 1 Mr Jones gave some students a mental arithmetic test. There were 15 questions. The results are shown in the table below:

Marks in test	Frequency		Marks in test	Frequency
0	1		8	6
1	0		9	4
2	1		10	7
3	0		11	6
4	2		12	10
5	3		13	8
6	3		14	7
7	4		15	4

a How many students took the mental arithmetic test?

b What percentage of students scored 10 or more marks in the mental arithmetic test?

The data is then put into a grouped frequency table.

Number of marks in mental arithmetic test	Frequency
0–3	
4–7	
8–11	
12–15	

c Copy and complete the frequency table.

d Give one advantage of using the original frequency table. AO3

e Give one advantage of using the grouped frequency table.

EQ **2** William measured the height, to the nearest centimetre, of 20 people. His results are listed below:

140, 143, 147, 147, 150, 150, 151, 154, 155, 156, 158, 159, 161, 162, 165, 166, 167, 170, 174, 177

Height (h) in cm	Frequency
$140 \leqslant h < 150$	
$150 \leqslant h < 160$	
$160 \leqslant h < 170$	
$170 \leqslant h < 180$	

a Copy and complete the grouped frequency table.

b How many people are over 160 cm tall?

c How many people had a height of less than 150 cm?

d Which group would someone with a height of 170 cm go in?

EQ **3** Molly measured the masses, to the nearest kilogram, of some students. Her results are listed below:

47   47   48   50   51   51   54   57   58   58   59   60

61   64   64   64   67   67   69   70   72   73   74

a Copy and complete the grouped frequency table.

Masses (m) in kg	Frequency
$45 \leqslant m < 50$	
$50 \leqslant m < 55$	
$55 \leqslant m < 60$	
$60 \leqslant m < 65$	
$65 \leqslant m < 70$	
$70 \leqslant m < 75$	

b How many people had a mass of less than 60 kg?

c Which group would someone with a height of 55 kg go into?

Grade 4

4 Pedro collected data about the pocket money that the other students in his class received in one week. His results are listed below. All the amounts are in euros. AO2

5.00   11.25   6.65   8.80   12.00   13.20   13.55   12.80

8.50   12.25   5.00   10.00   14.40   9.80   10.20   7.80

15.00   10.45   6.30   9.60   11.60   10.00   8.70   6.75

Design a grouped frequency table to illustrate this data.

Choose your class limits class so that you have four or five equal intervals.

5 Some books were weighed. This is the list of their weights to the nearest gram.

52	43	44	34
23	26	27	29
24	21	37	39
29	30	37	47
41	43	44	20

a Copy and complete the grouped frequency table.

Weight w (nearest gram)	Tally	Frequency
$20 \leqslant w < 25$		
$25 \leqslant w < 30$		
$30 \leqslant w < 35$		
$35 \leqslant w < 40$		
$40 \leqslant w < 45$		
$45 \leqslant w < 50$		
$50 \leqslant w < 55$		

b How many books weighed less than 30 grams?

c In which class interval are the most books?

d Give one disadvantage of grouping data in this way.

To simplify the data the 20 values are regrouped as shown.

Weight w (nearest gram)	Tally	Frequency
$20 \leqslant w < 30$		
$30 \leqslant w < 40$		
$40 \leqslant w < 50$		

e Give two reasons why the first table is a better form of grouping than the second. **AO3**

6 The table shows the time to the nearest minute for some students to complete a piece of homework.

Time, t (minutes)	Frequency
0–19	3
20–24	5
25–29	7
30–34	10
35–49	4
50–	2

a What are the class limits of the second class interval?

  i Lower limit

  ii Upper limit

b Why has the table got a class interval 50– ?

c Write down one reason why the class intervals are of varying width.

d Mrs Roberts believes that the students should be able to complete the homework   **AO2**
in under 35 minutes. Does the table support her belief? Give a reason for your answer.

2.3 Two-way tables

Quick reminder

A two-way table lets you show two variables at the same time.

Exercise 2C

Grade 3

 1 The two-way table shows the number of slices of toast and the number of sausages that 40 students bought at breakfast one morning in the school canteen.

		Number of slices of toast			
		0	**1**	**2**	**3**
Number of sausages	**0**	5	7	2	1
	1	1	12	4	2
	2	2	2	1	1

a How many students bought two sausages and three slices of toast?

b How many students bought exactly one sausage?

c How many students bought at least one slice of toast?

d Look at the '5' in the table. How does the breakfast of these five students differ from the other 35 students in the table?   **AO2**

 2 The two-way table shows the hair colour and gender of students in Mr Khan's tutor group.   **AO2**

		Hair colour				
		Brown	**Blonde**	**Black**	**Ginger/auburn**	**Total**
Gender	**Boys**	6	7	3	0	16
	Girls	7	4	1	2	14
	Total	13	11	4	2	30

a How many girls have black hair?

b How many boys have blonde hair?

c How many girls have neither brown nor black hair?

d What is the least frequent hair colour?

e How many students are in Mr Khan's tutor group?

There are 32 students in Mr Alam's tutor group. Two boys and one girl have ginger/auburn hair.

f Compare percentage of students in Mr Khan's tutor group who have ginger/auburn hair with those in Mr Alam's group.

3 The two-way table shows the number of televisions per house of 30 houses on a street and the number of cars per house. No household has more than three televisions or three cars.

AO2

	0 televisions	1 televisions	2 televisions	3 televisions
0 cars	1	1	2	0
1 car	0	3	5	1
2 cars	0	4	5	2
3 cars	0	1	3	2

a How many houses have exactly three cars and two televisions?

b How many houses have three cars?

c How many houses have two televisions?

d Jess says that someone living in this street is more likely to have one car and one television than three cars and three televisions. Explain why Jess is correct.

Grade 4

4 100 students at Hightown School each study one of three option subjects.

The two-way table shows some information about these students.

	RS	German	History	Total
Female	35			53
Male		17		47
Total	47	22		100

a Copy and complete the two-way table.

b How many male students study History?   AO2

c How many female students study German?   AO2

d How many students study History?   AO2

e At Newtown School 54 girls out of a sample of 150 students study RS. Determine which school, Hightown or Newtown has the higher percentage of female students studying RS.

5 The two-way table gives some information about the lunch arrangements of 60 students.

	School lunch	Packed lunch	Other	Total
Female			6	32
Male	21	7		
Total	38			60

a Copy and complete the two-way table.

b How many female students have a packed lunch?   AO2

c How many male students do not have a school lunch or packed lunch?   AO2

d How many students have a packed lunch?   AO2

e What fraction of students have something other than a school or packed lunch?

EQ **6** Alice is collecting some information as to whether the students in two classes watched football on television yesterday. **AO2**

There are 61 students in total.

29 of the students are male.

24 females watched football.

8 boys did not watch football.

a Use this information to copy and complete the two-way table.

	Male	Female	Total
Watched football			
Did not watch football			
Total			

b How many female students did not watch football?

c How many students did not watch football?

d What percentage of male students did watch football?

e Alice says that her results show that football is more popular with females than with males. Discuss whether Alice's conclusion is valid. **AO2**

2.4 Pictograms, line graphs and bar graphs

Quick reminder

A **pictogram** is a frequency table in which frequency is represented by a repeated symbol. The symbol itself usually represents a number of items, but can also represent just a single unit. The key tells you how many items are represented by a symbol.

A **bar chart** consists of a series of bars or blocks of the same width, drawn either vertically or horizontally from an axis. The heights or lengths of the bars always represent frequencies.

Line graphs are usually used to show how data changes over time. One such use is to indicate trends, for example, whether the Earth's temperature is increasing as the concentration of carbon dioxide builds up in the atmosphere, or whether a firm's profit margin is falling year-on-year.

Exercise 2D

Grade 1

  Questions 1 and 2 relate to the data in the table below, which shows the number of cars caught speeding while driving past Frank's school last week.

Day	Mon	Tue	Wed	Thu	Fri	Sat	Sun
Frequency	70	59	41	20	40	52	21

a Draw a pictogram to illustrate this data. Use a key of one car-shaped symbol to equal 20 cars.

b Explain why a key of one symbol to equal 2 cars is not a good idea. **AO3**

  a Draw a suitable bar chart to illustrate this data.

b Explain why you think Monday had the most cars caught speeding and why the numbers on Tuesday, Wednesday and Thursday went down. **AO3**

c Give one advantage of drawing a bar chart rather than a pictogram for this data. **AO3**

Grade 2

EQ **3** For her business plan, Michelle has produced a bar chart to compare the average number of flowers sold per week in her shop over the last two years.

AO2

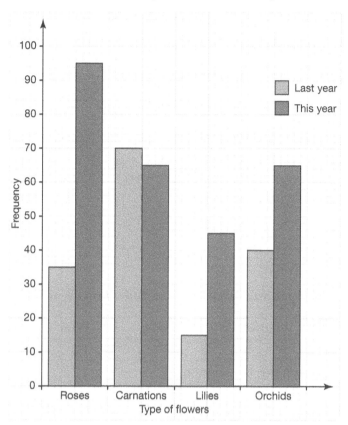

a Which flower was most popular last year?

b Which flower was most popular this year?

c How many roses were sold last year?

d How many more lilies were sold this year than last year?

EQ **4** The pictogram below shows the number of text messages received by four friends last week.

AO2

Name		Number of texts received
Jason		
Amir		
Glynis		10
Aisha		8
	Total	

Key: = 5 text messages.

a How many texts did Amir receive?

b Copy and complete the pictogram.

c How many texts did the four friends receive altogether?

d Glynis said that she received 20% of the texts sent. Show that she is correct. **AO2**

2.5 Pie charts

Quick reminder

Each category of data is represented by a sector of the pie chart. The angle of each sector is proportional to the frequency of the category it represents.

A pie chart cannot show individual frequencies, like a bar chart can. It can only show proportions.

Exercise 2E

Grade 3

1 The table shows the favourite ice cream flavours of students in the school canteen.

Flavour	Vanilla	Strawberry	Toffee	Plain	Other
Frequency	32	6	17	3	2

Draw a pie chart to represent this information.

2 The pie chart below shows the proportions of the different number of sick days   **AO2**
taken by 48 staff in the same company last year.

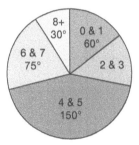

a What is the angle of the sector representing 2 and 3 sick days off?

b How many people took 4 or 5 sick days off?

3 The information below is on numbers of fish in a canal.

Fish	Frequency
Trout	50
Perch	64
Carp	29
Roach	37

Draw a pie chart to represent this information

Grade 4

4 In a survey, people were asked to name their favourite biscuit. The results are shown in the table and pie chart below. **AO2**

Biscuit	Frequency	Angle
Bourbon	12	
Oreo	18	90
Hobnob		80
Digestive	19	
Rich Tea		35

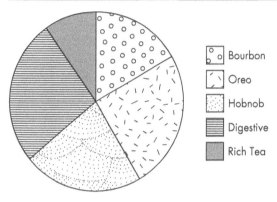

Use the pie chart to complete the table.

Grade 6

5 The proportions of elm, beech and oak trees in Greg's Wood, in 1955 and 1995, are shown in the pie charts below. **AO2**

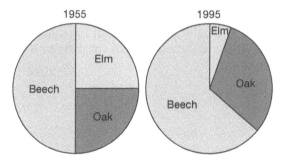

In the period from 1955 to 1995, most elm trees in Wales were killed by a fungus.

a Write down one feature shown in the pie charts that suggests that Greg's Wood could be in Wales.

Glynis says, 'These pie charts show that the number of beech trees in Greg's Wood has increased in the period from 1955 to 1995.'

b Glynis is **wrong**. Explain why.

2.6 Comparative pie charts

Quick reminder

Comparative pie charts are used to compare sets of data. The frequencies are proportional to the areas of the pie charts.

If r_1 and r_2 are the radii of pie charts 1 and 2 and f_1 and f_2 are the frequencies, then

$$r_2 = r_1 \frac{\sqrt{f_2}}{\sqrt{f_1}}$$

Exercise 2F

Grade 7

1   A computer company's profits increase from £1 230 000 in 2010 to £1 345 000 in 2011. Sue is asked to draw two comparative pie charts to illustrate this increase. If she chooses a radius of 25 cm for the 2011 graph, calculate the radius she should use for the 2010 graph.

2   The table below gives information about the number of people living in two small villages.

Llanegwad			Llanarthne	
Age	Frequency		Age	Frequency
0–18	5		0–18	15
19–37	14		19–37	44
38–56	12		38–56	77
57–75	10		57–75	28
75+	4		75+	16

Using a radius of 2 cm for Llanegwad, draw comparative pie charts to compare the ages of the people in the two villages.

(EQ) 3   The comparative pie charts below show information about the number of people living in a town who smoked in 2000 and the number of smokers in 2018.

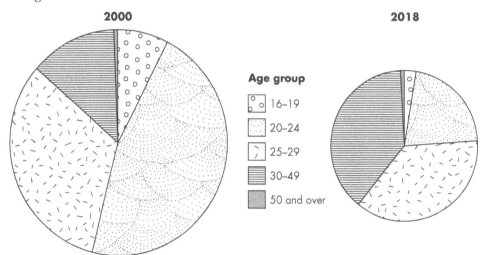

2000　　　　　　　　　　　　**2018**

Age group
- 16–19
- 20–24
- 25–29
- 30–49
- 50 and over

a   What has happened to the total number of people who smoke? Explain how the charts show this.　　AO2

b   Write down the age group with the greatest change. Is this an increase or a decrease?

c   If there were 1500 smokers in 2000 how many were there in 2018?

4 Hannah draws two comparative pie charts to show how much money she spent on items of clothing in 2017 and 2018. She spent £2560 on clothes in 2017 and the pie chart she draws has a radius of 1.5 cm. If the 2018 pie chart has a radius of 2 cm, calculate how much money she spent in 2018. **AO2**

5 A shoe shop's profits decrease from £420 000 in 2016 to £270 000 in 2018. Angharad is asked to draw two comparative pie charts to illustrate the drop in profits. If she chooses a radius of 5 cm for the 2016 graph, calculate the radius she should use for the 2018 graph.

2.7 Misleading graphs

Quick reminder

Think about the reasons why someone would want to produce a misleading graph.

Consider whether the vertical axis on a chart or graph is correct.

If images are used, are they in proportion or are they purposely misleading?

Exercise 2G

Grade 3

1 The graph below shows the favourite types of TV programmes when 250 students were surveyed. **AO3**

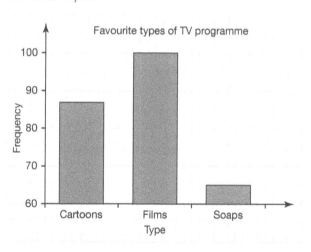

a Explain what is misleading about the graph.

b Redraw the graph to make it less misleading.

2 The graph below shows the changes in petrol prices over a four-year period. **AO3**

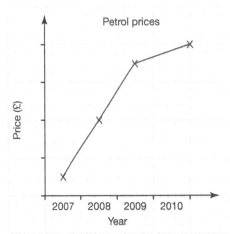

Explain what is misleading about the graph.

EQ **3** This graph appeared in a fishing magazine. **AO3**
Number of fishing licences sold.

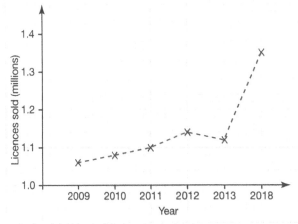

Give two reasons why the graph is misleading.

4 The table below shows the number of shoes sold in a shoe shop last week.

Day	Mon	Tue	Wed	Thu	Fri	Sat	Sun
Number of shoes sold	22	19	18	24	34	46	21

a Draw this information in a bar chart to make it a misleading bar chart. **AO2**

b Explain what your bar chart shows to someone who is not good at spotting a misleading bar chart. **AO3**

5 The table below shows the amount of petrol sold at a petrol station last week.

Day	Mon	Tue	Wed	Thu	Fri
Petrol sold (× 1000 litres)	400	340	200	180	550

a Draw this information in a line graph to make it look as though no petrol was sold on Thursday. **AO2**

b Explain how you made the line graph look misleading. **AO3**

6 Craig puts an advert in a local newspaper to encourage more customers to his shop. AO3

He counts the number of customers the week before, the week during and the week after the advert is in the paper.

He draws this accurate 3D pie chart to show the results.

Number of customers

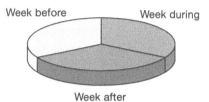

Week before Week during

Week after

Craig says 'look at the pie chart! It is obvious that the advert was a success.'

Explain why this pie chart is misleading and shows that Craig is **wrong**.

7 AO3

a Explain why this advertisement might be misleading.

b Which jar is the better value?

2.8 Choropleth maps

Quick reminder

Choropleth maps are maps in which areas are shaded differently, to illustrate a distribution.

Every map should have a 'key' that makes sense of the data. Remember to study this carefully before answering a question.

Exercise 2H

Grade 4

 1 Part of a coral reef is subdivided into square sections.

The number of different species of fish passing each square in an hour is shown in the table below.

24	20	23	22	18	19
26	23	19	21	10	18
39	33	30	22	9	6
25	21	24	21	17	19

a Use the key to produce a choropleth map illustrating the data.   AO2

Key

 0–10   11–20   21–30   31–40

b Part of the coral reef has been damaged by fishermen using dynamite.

Draw a line around the area where you think the coral has been damaged.

c Explain your answer to part **b**.

d One area is regularly visited by divers who feed the fish they see.

Draw a line around this area.

e Explain your answer to part **d**.

2 A forest is subdivided into square sections.

The number of different species of birds in each section is shown in each square of the table below.

10	6	3	3	3	9
13	12	4	4	10	11
11	19	14	12	14	13
15	19	12	12	12	10

a Use the key to produce a choropleth map illustrating the data.   AO2

Key

 0–5   6–10   11–15   16–20

b Part of the forest has been cut down and the trees removed for their wood.

Draw a line around the area where you think the trees have been cut down and removed.

c Explain your answer to part **b**.

d One area of the forest has very fertile soil and a lot of trees grow there.

Draw a line around this area.

EQ 3

The choropleth map shows the percentage change of population in Scotland from 2008 to 2009.

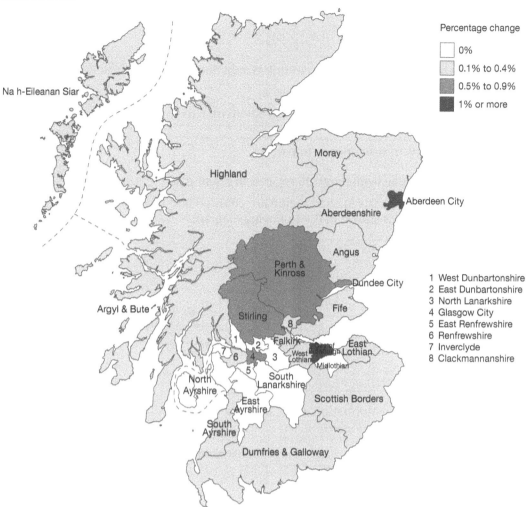

Percentage change

☐ 0%
▢ 0.1% to 0.4%
▨ 0.5% to 0.9%
■ 1% or more

1 West Dunbartonshire
2 East Dunbartonshire
3 North Lanarkshire
4 Glasgow City
5 East Renfrewshire
6 Renfrewshire
7 Inverclyde
8 Clackmannanshire

a Which region has the highest population change?   AO2

b Give a reason for your answer to part **a**.

c What is the percentage population change of Inverclyde?

d How could you improve on the way the information is displayed on this map?   AO3

4 Each dot on the diagram below represents a child playing in the school playground.

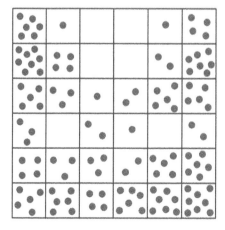

a Use the key to produce a choropleth map illustrating the data. **AO2**

Key

b Someone has thrown a stink bomb. Put a cross (X) where you think it landed.

c Explain your answer to part **b**.

d Draw an arrow on your choropleth map to show which way you think the wind is blowing.

e Explain your answer to part **d**.

EQ **5** A forest is divided into 16 regions of equal size.

The owls' nests in each region are counted and the numbers are written in the squares, as shown in the following diagram.

0	1	0	0
2	3	6	2
1	5	8	1
0	1	1	2

Key | 2 | means there are two owls' nests in this region

a Use the information in the diagram to copy and complete this choropleth map.

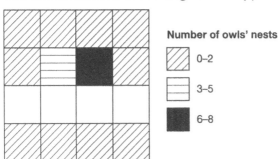

Number of owls' nests

0–2

3–5

6–8

b Describe how the owls' nests are spread across the forest. **AO2**

2.9 Stem-and-leaf diagrams

Quick reminder

The numbers in a stem-and-leaf diagram may be left in the order in which they are given, but it is usual to rearrange them, to give an **ordered** stem-and-leaf diagram. The diagrams can be used to find measures such as the range and the median.

Exercise 2I

Grade 4

 1 21 students try to guess when 10 seconds is up by pressing a computer key. **AO2**
Their actual times are shown below:

10.8	11.4	9.7	11.5	10.5	11.3	11.1
12.3	10.9	11.5	10.6	10.8	12.0	11.3
11.6	11.5	12.1	10.6	10.9	11.1	11.9

a Construct a stem-and-leaf diagram to illustrate the data.

b Construct an ordered stem-and-leaf diagram to illustrate the data.

c Find the range.

d Write down the median value.

2 The masses of 31 tomatoes, in grams, are shown below: **AO2**

Stem	Leaf
2	9 7 5 6
3	5 4 6 6 7 0 1 4 5 6 3
4	0 1 4 1 7 6 2 7 8
5	3 8 0 2 9
6	1 2

a Construct an ordered stem-and-leaf diagram.

b Write down a key

c How heavy is the lightest tomato?

d What does the heaviest tomato weigh?

e What is the range of this data?

f Use your stem-and-leaf diagram to work out the median.

3 The back-to-back stem-and-leaf diagram below shows the times taken in seconds **AO2**
to complete a puzzle successfully by two groups of different ages.

Adults	Stem	14–16 year olds
8	2	0 1
8 4	3	0 4 9
9 4 2	4	5 6 7 7 7 8 8
7 4 0 0	5	3 4 5 7 8
8 8 7 5 3 1	6	0 2 4
7 6 6 5 4	7	3 7
7 4 3 2	8	2 4
4 4 2	9	2

Key: 3|4 means 34 seconds

a What was the shortest time taken by the 14–16 year olds?

b What was the longest time taken by the adults?

c Write down the median values of both data sets.

d Comment on how well each group performed.

A nurse took the pulse rate of 23 patients.

The pulse rates are shown in the stem-and-leaf-diagram.

Pulse rates

6	7 8
7	2 3 4 4
7	5 5 5 5 8 9
8	0 2 3 3 4
8	8 8 9
9	0 4 4

Key: 6|7 means 67 beats per minute

a Write down the median pulse rate.

b Write down the mode pulse rates.

The sum of all the pulse rates was 1840.

c Work out the mean pulse rate.

The nurse recorded the pulse rates of the same 23 patients just after each of them had woken up. The median was 75, the mean was 76 and the range was 29.

d Compare the pulse rates just after waking with those taken in the middle of   AO2
the day.

e Explain why a stem-and-leaf diagram is an appropriate way to show this data.   AO3
Describe how the diagram could be adapted to show the pulse rates after
waking up.

2.10 Histograms and frequency polygons

Histograms look similar to bar graphs but there are no gaps between the bars. They are represented in two formats: equal class-width intervals and unequal class-width intervals.

Frequency polygons are often used instead of histograms to compare two sets of data. Each point is plotted in the centre of the group and the points are joined up using a straight line.

Cumulative frequency step polygons are drawn using discrete data. Points are joined horizontally and vertically, i.e. in steps. The points are not joined diagonally as in a cumulative frequency curve or polygon because the data is discrete.

Quick reminder

Exercise 2J

Grade 3

1 The table below shows a grouped frequency distribution of the marks that a class of students achieved in their Spanish exam.

Spanish result (%)	40–45	46–50	51–55	56–60	61–65
Number of students	2	5	9	8	4

a Draw a frequency diagram to illustrate the results.

b Draw a frequency polygon on the same diagram.

2 A magazine carried out a survey of the ages of its readers.

The table shows the results of the survey.

Age, y (years)	Frequency
$5 \leqslant y < 15$	8
$15 \leqslant y < 25$	39
$25 \leqslant y < 35$	30
$35 \leqslant y < 45$	15
$45 \leqslant y < 55$	8

a Draw a frequency polygon for this data.

b The magazine editor is thinking of including an article about buying antiques. **AO3**
Do you think this is a good idea? Explain your answer.

3 The frequency polygon shows the ages of some people who attended a charity **AO2**
fun run.

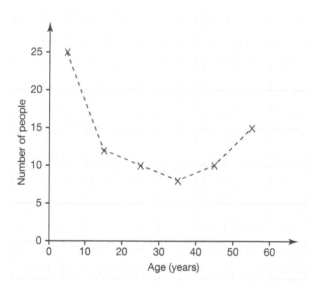

Hamish said, 'most of the fun runners were 5 years old'.

Explain why this might be wrong.

Grade 6

4 The table below shows the grades achieved by Year 10 pupils in their examinations.

Grade	4	5	6	7	8	9
Frequency	12	16	25	27	15	9

  a Draw a cumulative frequency step polygon to illustrate the data.

  b Use your graph to find the median grade and the grades between which the interquartile range lies.

5 Linda uses the following table to record the number of goals scored in a local football league.

Number of goals	0	1	2	3	4	5
Frequency	5	18	26	15	6	2

  a Draw a cumulative frequency step polygon to illustrate the data.

  b Find the median and interquartile range of the data.

6 Sue records the number of people travelling in 50 cars in the table below.

Number of people	Frequency
1	8
2	17
3	12
4	10
5	3

  a Draw a cumulative frequency step polygon to illustrate the data.

  b Find the median and interquartile range of the data.

Grade 7

7 The mass, in kg, of the suitcases on a plane are shown below:

12.7	10.4	16.0	16.0	12.8	15.2
19.1	14.0	14.8	16.0	16.7	15.1
10.1	15.3	11.2	12.6	18.3	11.6
17.6	13.3	10.3	19.3	11.6	15.3
19.2	14.5	17.0	15.1	15.1	18.4
16.0	16.3	12.2	16.1	11.7	16.7
10.2	15.3	15.2	13.3	15.5	15.8

  a Copy and complete the frequency table.

Mass, m	Tally	Frequency
$10 \leqslant m < 12$		
$12 \leqslant m < 14$		
$14 \leqslant m < 16$		
$16 \leqslant m < 18$		
$18 \leqslant m < 20$		

b Draw a histogram to illustrate the data.

c Write down the modal class.

d In which group does the median lie?

EQ **8** The number of merits gained by Year 9 students are summarised in the table below: **AO2**

Number of merits, m	Frequency
$0 \leqslant m < 20$	24
$20 \leqslant m < 40$	52
$40 \leqslant m < 60$	40
$60 \leqslant m < 90$	33
$90 \leqslant m < 150$	15

a Draw a histogram for this data.

b Any student with more than 80 merits gets to go on a school trip.
Last year there were 179 students in Year 9. 32 of these went on a school trip. **AO2**
Show that the percentage of Year 9 students going on a trip this year is lower
than last year.

EQ **9** The distances travelled by 100 different cars, each using 1 litre of petrol, are shown in
the following histogram and table.

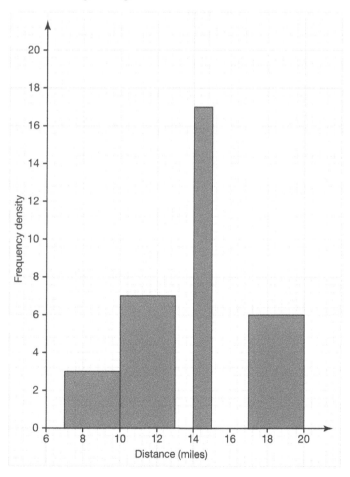

Distance (miles)	7–10	10–13	13–14	14–15	15–17	17–20
Frequency	9		18		17	

a Copy and complete the histogram and the table.

b Estimate the percentage of cars that travel between 12 and 16 miles on 1 litre of petrol.   **AO2**

The distances travelled by 200 vans, each using 1 litre of diesel fuel, are shown in the following histogram and table.

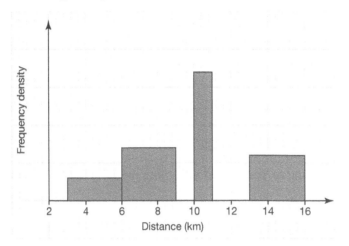

Distance (km)	3–6	6–9	9–10	10–11	11–13	13–16
Frequency	18		36		34	
Frequency density						

c Copy and complete the table.

d Copy and complete the histogram by drawing the two missing bars.

e Compare the percentage of cars and vans that travel between 12 and 16 km on 1 litre of fuel.   **AO2**

2.11 Cumulative frequency graphs

Quick reminder

A cumulative frequency graph can be used to find the interquartile range and the median.

Exercise 2K

Grade 6

 1. 160 students took a test. The cumulative frequency graph shows information about their marks.

AO2

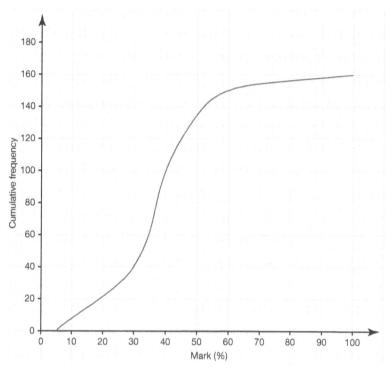

Work out an estimate for the interquartile range of their marks.

2. At a fundraising event, a game consists of spinning two large spinners and adding the scores. The results of the first 140 people to play the game are recorded in the table below.

AO2

Spinner score, s	Frequency
$1 \leqslant s < 20$	11
$21 \leqslant s < 40$	21
$41 \leqslant s < 60$	55
$61 \leqslant s < 80$	27
$81 \leqslant s < 100$	18
$101 \leqslant s < 120$	8

a. Draw a cumulative frequency diagram to show the data.

b. Use your diagram to estimate the median score.

c. Use your diagram to estimate the interquartile score.

d. Those who score more than 90 win a prize. What fraction of the people get a prize?

e. Those who score less than 30 are given another turn. Approximately what percentage of the people are allowed to spin again?

3 Jordan records the number of goals scored in his school's football league using the table below.

Number of goals	0	1	2	3	4	5	6
Frequency	7	10	24	25	10	6	2

a Draw a cumulative frequency step polygon to illustrate the data.

b Find the median of the data.

c Find the interquartile range of the data.

EQ **4** The lengths, in seconds, of 40 burps in a burping competition were recorded. **AO2**
A cumulative frequency diagram of this data is shown on the grid below.

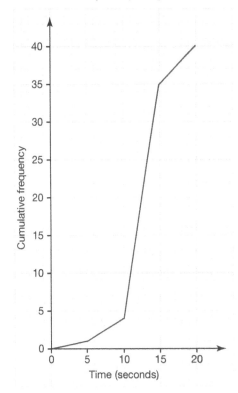

Use the diagram to find the limits between which the middle 50% of the times lie.

Grade 7

EQ **5** For 100 days Gemma kept a record of how late her bus was.
The information is shown in the following table.

Time late, t (mins)	Frequency
$0 \leqslant t \leqslant 2$	23
$2 < t \leqslant 4$	35
$4 < t \leqslant 6$	24
$6 < t \leqslant 8$	12
$8 < t \leqslant 10$	5
$10 < t \leqslant 12$	1

a Copy and complete the cumulative frequency table.

Time late, t (mins)	Cumulative frequency
$0 \leqslant t \leqslant 2$	
$2 < t \leqslant 4$	
$4 < t \leqslant 6$	
$6 < t \leqslant 8$	
$8 < t \leqslant 10$	
$10 < t \leqslant 12$	

b Using the information in your table, draw a cumulative frequency diagram.

c Use your cumulative frequency diagram to find an estimate for the median time that the bus was late.

d The bus company claims that the bus is no more than five minutes late 75% of the time. Do Gemma's results support this claim? Justify your answer.　AO2

2.12 Population pyramids

Quick reminder

Population pyramids look like back to back horizontal bar graphs and are used to compare percentages of populations by age and gender.

Exercise 2L

Grade 4

1 The populations of France and India are illustrated in the population pyramids below.　AO2

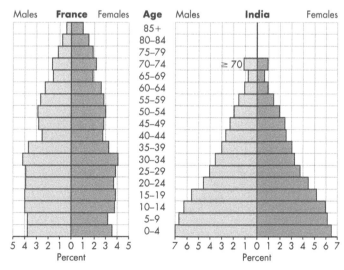

a Which age group had the largest percentage of males in France?

b Compare the populations of France and India.

2 The populations of the USA and Nigeria are illustrated in the population pyramids below.   AO2

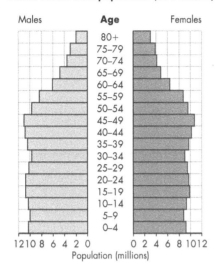
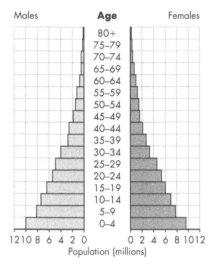

a Which age group has the largest population in Nigeria?

b Estimate the percentages of males aged between 15 and 19 in the USA.

c Compare the two populations.

3 The population of China in 2018 and the estimated population in 2050 are illustrated in the population pyramids below.   AO2

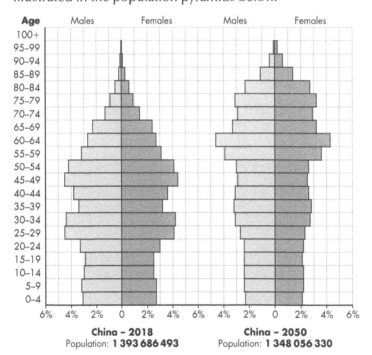

a Describe what is happening to the population.

b What can you say about the age of the population in 2050?

4 The population of Europeans and the population of Maoris in New Zealand are illustrated in the diagrams below.   AO2

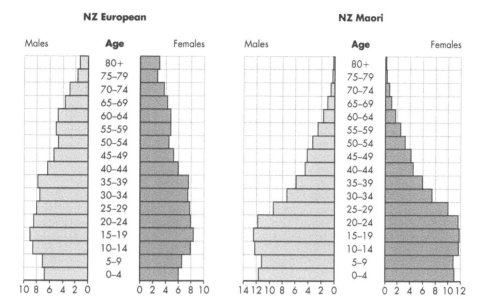

a Estimate the percentage of 15–19-year-old females of European origin in New Zealand.

b In what age group are 10% of Maoris female?

c Compare the populations.

5 The populations of Kenya, USA and Italy are illustrated below.

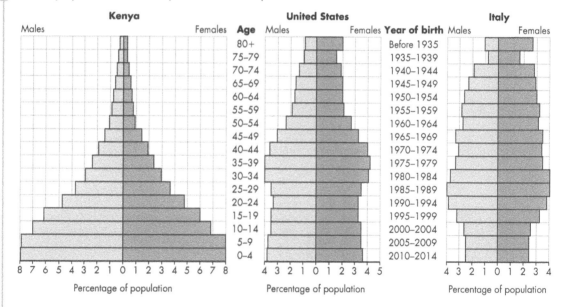

a Compare the three populations   AO2

b Which country and age group has the greatest percentage difference between males and females?

3 Summarising data

3.1 The mode

Quick reminder

The **mode** of a list of data is the number that occurs most often. So, for a frequency distribution, the mode is the number with the highest frequency.

Exercise 3A

Grade 2

1 The table below shows the number of goals scored last season by a football team.   AO2

Number of goals	0	1	2	3	4	5	6	7
Frequency	8	15	12	5	2	0	0	1

What was the modal number of goals scored?

2 This bar chart shows the number of bedrooms in the houses in a street.   AO2

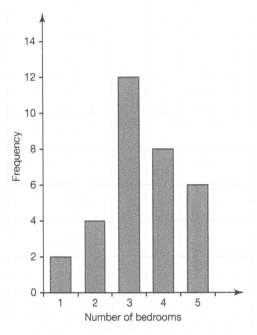

There are four two-bedroom houses.

What is the modal number of bedrooms?

3 Six numbers add up to 30. Two of the numbers are both 5.

If the mode of the six numbers is 4, what are the six numbers?

AO2

4 The stem-and-leaf diagram shows the mass of young mice in a pet shop.

```
4 | 6  6  8
5 | 0  0  2  5  5  6  8  9
6 | 1  2  3  3  4  8  8  8  9
7 | 0  2  2  5  5  5  5  7  9
8 | 0  3  4
```

Key: 5|0 means 50 g

Write down the modal mass.

Grade 4

EQ **5** The following table shows the height of seedlings in a greenhouse.

Height, h (cm)	Frequency
$10 \leqslant h < 12$	16
$12 \leqslant h < 14$	41
$14 \leqslant h < 16$	36
$16 \leqslant h < 18$	34
$18 \leqslant h < 20$	12

a Write down the modal class.

b Sam wants to draw a diagram that will show the modal class clearly. What kind of diagram should he draw? Justify your answer.

AO3

3.2 The median

Quick reminder

The median of a list of data arranged in ascending or descending order is the middle number.

When there is an even number of data items find the middle pair, add them together and divide by two.

If there are n items in a list, the position of the median can be found by working out $\frac{n+1}{2}$,

i.e. the median is the $\frac{n+1}{2}$ th item in the list.

Exercise 3B

Grade 3

1 The table below shows the number of goals conceded by a hockey team last season.

AO2

Number of goals	0	1	2	3	4	5
Frequency	11	8	3	1	0	1

What is:

a The modal number of goals?

b The median number of goals?

2 Ben works as a waiter. One Saturday night, he records the total bill for each table he serves and puts the information in this stem-and-leaf table: AO2

Stem		Leaf
2		8 9
3		1 3 3 5 7 8
4		2 2 5 6 9 9 9
5		3 4 4 6
6		2 8
7		1 2 2

Key: 2|8 represents £28

a How many tables did he serve?

b What was the modal bill?

c Find the median bill.

Grade 4

3 Five numbers have a mode of 4 and a median of 6.   AO2

Write down any of the five numbers you can and explain what you can tell about the value of the others.

4 Six friends compare their pocket money.   AO2

The median is £6.50.

What can you tell about the third and fourth largest amounts of pocket money?

EQ **5** A survey was done to count the number of eggs in sparrows' nests in two different regions. Each region had the same area.

The data have been recorded in this table.

Number of eggs	Frequency: region A	Frequency: region B
4	7	3
5	14	7
6	15	18
7	9	23
8	4	20
9	1	6
Total		

a Write down the median number of eggs counted in a nest in region A.

b Write down the median number of eggs counted in a nest in region B.

c Which region, A or B, do you think is nearest to easily available food? Explain your answer.   AO2

(EQ) 6 The table gives information about the neck sizes, in inches, of 20 shirts.

Neck size (inches)	Frequency
14	2
$14\frac{1}{2}$	7
15	6
$15\frac{1}{2}$	5

a Write down the modal neck size.

b Work out the median neck size.

c Work out the mean neck size.

d Which average would best describe the neck sizes of the 20 shirts? Give a reason for your answer.   AO3

3.3 The mean

Quick reminder

$$\text{Mean} = \frac{\text{sum of all the values}}{\text{total number of values}}$$

$$\text{Mean of a frequency distribution} = \frac{\Sigma fx}{\Sigma f}$$

Exercise 3C

Grade 2

1 Four boys are collecting conkers. The mean number of conkers they have is 7.   AO2

   a What is the total number of conkers the four boys have?

   b A fifth boy who only has two conkers joins them. What is the total number of conkers they have between the five of them?

   c What is the mean number of conkers for the five boys?

2 Ariba goes on holiday for 7 days. The mean maximum temperature for the first 6 days is 89°F.   AO2

   The maximum temperature on the last day is 103°F.

   What is the mean maximum temperature for the whole week?

Grade 4

3 For each of the frequency tables below, calculate the mean:

a

x	4	5	6	7
f	1	3	4	2

b

x	20	40	60	80	100
f	2	5	8	3	2

c

x	20	25	30	35	40	45
f	1	3	3	1	0	2

4 Joon does a survey to see how many text messages people send.
He asks 100 students how many texts they sent yesterday evening.

The results are shown in this table.

Number of texts	Frequency
0	6
1	25
2	31
3	24
4	14

Calculate the mean.

5 A town planner counts the number of people in 80 cars in a traffic survey.

The results are shown in this table.

Number of people	Frequency
1	3
2	21
3	18
4	20
5	12
6	2
7	3
8	1

Calculate:

a the mean

b the mode

c the median.

Grade 5

EQ **6** A survey was done to count the number of eggs in sparrows' nests.

The data has been recorded in the following table.

Number of eggs (x)	Frequency (f)	fx
4	7	28
5	14	70
6	15	90
7	9	
8	4	
9	1	
Total		

Work out the mean number of eggs.

Give your answer correct to 1 decimal place.

3.4 Averages from grouped data

Quick reminder

When you use mean $= \frac{\Sigma fx}{\Sigma f}$ for a grouped frequency table, you must use the mid-points of each class as your values of x. This gives an estimate of the mean.
If all the classes have the same width, the modal class is the class with the highest frequency.

Exercise 3D

Grade 4

 1 The following table gives information about the length of time a random selection of 60 people took to text the sentence:

'The quick brown fox jumped over the lazy dog.'

Time taken, x (seconds)	Number of people	Mid-point value	
$20 \leqslant x < 30$	18	25	
$30 \leqslant x < 40$	12		
$40 \leqslant x < 50$	6		
$50 \leqslant x < 60$	24		
		Total	

a Copy and complete the table.

b Estimate the mean time taken.

c Explain why your answer to part b is only an estimate.   AO3

 2 Calculate an estimate of the mean of each of these grouped frequency tables, where x is a continuous variable.

Give your answers correct to 3 significant figures where necessary.

a

Class	Frequency
$1 \leqslant x < 5$	1
$5 \leqslant x < 9$	3
$9 \leqslant x < 13$	7
$13 \leqslant x < 17$	2
$17 \leqslant x \leqslant 21$	2

b

Class	Frequency
$10 \leqslant x < 20$	18
$20 \leqslant x < 30$	13
$30 \leqslant x < 40$	7
$40 \leqslant x < 50$	4
$50 \leqslant x \leqslant 60$	1

c

Class	Frequency
$1 \leqslant x < 5$	1
$5 \leqslant x < 10$	17
$10 \leqslant x < 15$	20
$15 \leqslant x < 20$	10
$20 \leqslant x \leqslant 25$	20

3 The amounts spent by 30 customers at a supermarket were recorded and the following table was produced:

Amount spent, £x	Frequency
$0 < x \leqslant 20$	12
$20 < x \leqslant 40$	7
$40 < x \leqslant 60$	6
$60 < x \leqslant 80$	5

a Write down the modal class.

b Calculate an estimate of the mean.

4 The amounts spent by 40 customers at a supermarket were recorded and the following table was produced:

Amount owing, £x	Frequency
$0 < x \leqslant 50$	2
$50 < x \leqslant 100$	13
$100 < x \leqslant 150$	15
$150 < x \leqslant 200$	6
$200 < x \leqslant 250$	3
$250 < x < 300$	1

Calculate an estimate of the mean.

5 50 students were asked how long they spent using a computer in one day.

The results were collected and presented in this table:

Length of time, t (hours)	Frequency
$0 < t \leqslant 2$	13
$2 < t \leqslant 4$	18
$4 < t \leqslant 6$	11
$6 < t \leqslant 8$	5
$8 < t \leqslant 10$	3

a Write down the modal class.

b Calculate an estimate of the mean.

6 100 students guess how long the headteacher's speech will last on Prize giving Day.

The guesses were grouped into the following table:

Length of time, t (mins)	Frequency
$0 < t \leqslant 4$	21
$4 < t \leqslant 8$	25
$8 < t \leqslant 12$	33
$12 < t \leqslant 16$	11
$16 < t \leqslant 20$	5
$20 < t \leqslant 24$	4
$24 < t \leqslant 28$	1

a Write down the modal class.

b Calculate an estimate of the mean.

7 Jess is investigating the length of books. She goes online and finds the number of pages in each of the week's top-selling books.

To present the data clearly, she puts the lengths into groups and produces the following table:

Number of pages, p	Frequency
$0 \leqslant p \leqslant 99$	12
$100 \leqslant p \leqslant 199$	37
$200 \leqslant p \leqslant 299$	33
$300 \leqslant p \leqslant 399$	18

Use Jess's table to estimate the mean.

8 Miss Spell records the marks that Year 9 get in their English exam and puts them in a table:

Marks, m	Frequency
11–20	1
21–30	0
31–40	26
41–50	29
51–60	34
61–70	12
71–80	2
81–90	1
91–100	1

Use the table to estimate the mean.

9 A doctor times how long 20 patients take to do a test on two consecutive days: **AO2**

Time, t (seconds)	$10 < t \leqslant 15$	$15 < t \leqslant 20$	$20 < t \leqslant 25$	$25 < t \leqslant 30$	$30 < t \leqslant 35$
Frequency: Day 1	1	4	5	7	3
Frequency: Day 2	5	5	2	7	1

He uses the table to estimate the mean time on each day.

On which day was the estimate of the mean time lower, and by how much?

Grade 5

10 Jane estimates the mean for a grouped frequency table. She rubs out one of **AO2**
the frequencies and gives the table to her friend Jo. She tells Jo that the estimate
of the mean was 8 and asks her to calculate the missing frequency.

Here is the table she gives to Jo:

t	$0 < t \leqslant 4$	$4 < t \leqslant 8$	$8 < t \leqslant 12$	$12 < t \leqslant 16$
Frequency	2		3	7

What is the missing frequency?

3.5 Which average?

Quick reminder

In certain circumstances, either the mean or the median or the mode can be a better 'average' to use than the other two. This may be because the person calculating the average wants to use it to prove something.

The mean can be affected badly by a few very large or very small items.

There can be more than one mode, or none.

The average should be representative of all the data.

In this exercise, give your answers correct to 3 significant figures where necessary.

Exercise 3E

Grade 3

1 A small firm employs 10 people. Their annual salaries are: **AO3**

£8000   £8000   £22000   £23000   £24000

£25500   £26000   £27500   £28000   £90000

What is:

a the mode

b the median

c the mean?

Which average would you say is most representative of this data and why are the
other two not as useful?

2 In Diana's class, 6 girls have brown eyes, 4 girls have blue eyes, 2 girls have green eyes and one has grey eyes.   AO3

Which is the only average you can find for the colour of these girls' eyes?

3 Donald uses a spell checker to correct the mistakes he has made in his English coursework.   AO3

The number of errors on each page is:

2 5 12 13 8 45 11 9 10

For these numbers of errors, calculate if possible:

a the mode

b the median

c the mean.

Giving reasons, say which of these averages best describes the data.

4 A chocolate manufacturer makes tubes containing small chocolate sweets.   AO3

It claims an average of 40 sweets in each tube.

Jerry decides to check this claim and counts the number of chocolates in 20 tubes with the following results:

Number of chocolates in a tube	Frequency
0	1
35	2
36	2
37	4
38	3
39	3
40	5

a For the number of chocolate sweets in a tube, calculate:

   i the mean

   ii the median

   iii the mode.

b Jerry then discovers that the empty tube had not originally been empty, but that the chocolates had been eaten by his little brother before Jerry could count them. He decides to discard this tube from his investigation and only use the data for the other 19 tubes.

   i How will this affect the three averages you have found?

   ii Which average is the manufacturer using and why?

(EQ) 5 Mr Truman's PE class and Mr Thom's PE class had a 'throw the cricket ball' competition.

The results are shown below.

Mr Truman's PE class: 31 m, 29 m, 47 m, 50 m, 27 m, 7 m, 33 m, 21 m, 37 m, 29 m, 47 m, 36 m, 22 m

Mr Thom's PE class: 36 m, 30 m, 33 m, 30 m, 37 m, 30 m, 35 m, 33 m, 31 m, 34 m

a Which 'average' best describes Mr Truman's PE class?   AO3

b Which 'average' best describes Mr Thom's PE class?

c Which class do you think is the best at throwing a cricket ball? Give a reason for your answer.   AO2

3.6 Data transformations

Quick reminder

If all data values are increased by the same amount, all averages are increased or decreased by this value.

Exercise 3F

Grade 5

1. Find the mean of the following data using an assumed mean of 36.

   25, 17, 28, 35, 38, 47, 49, 52, 55, 44, 39

2. Find the mean by transforming the data to make it easier to use.

   203, 207, 256, 229, 235, 241, 256, 223, 245, 267, 289

3. Describe what happens to the mean median and mode when each value in a data set is increased by the same number.

4. A teacher measures the height of seven pupils. The mean was 125 cm and the median was 121 cm. It was subsequently found that the teacher measured each child incorrectly increasing their height by 2 cm. What is the new mean and median height?

5. Jane's average earnings in 2017 were £3200 per month. In 2018 her earnings increased by 5%. Calculate her average earnings in 2018.

3.7 Geometric mean and weighted mean

Quick reminder

The geometric mean of n numbers is the nth root of their product.

So the geometric mean of 4 and 9 is $\sqrt{4 \times 9} = \sqrt{36} = 6$

and the geometric mean of 1, 2, 8 and 16 is $\sqrt[4]{1 \times 2 \times 8 \times 16} = \sqrt[4]{256} = 4$.

Usually the geometric mean will not be a whole number, so you should write down the first five figures of your answer and then round it to 3 significant figures (or whatever the question says).

e.g. the geometric mean of 2, 4 and 9 is $\sqrt[3]{2 \times 4 \times 9} = \sqrt[3]{72} = 4.1601 = 4.16$ (to 3 sig. fig.)

Weighted mean = $\dfrac{\Sigma(\text{value} \times \text{weighting})}{\Sigma \text{weightings}}$

Example

Steve is going to buy a new bike.

His criteria are:

Weight 40%; Cost 15%; Frame quality 30%; Brake performance 10%; Groupset 5%

A cycling magazine rates three bikes out of 10 for each of the criteria as follows:

Bike	Weight	Cost	Frame quality	Brake performance	Groupset
Colnago C64	6	5	10	4	9
Pinarello F10	8	7	7	6	7
De Rosa SK	7	9	8	5	8

Which bike should Steve buy?

Answer

$$\text{Weighted mean} = \frac{\Sigma(\text{value} \times \text{weighting})}{\Sigma \text{weightings}}$$

Bike	Colnago C64	Pinarello F10	DeRosa SK	Value × weightings Colnago C64	Value × weightings Pinarello F10	Value × weightings De Rosa SK
Weight	6	8	7	2.4	3.2	2.8
Cost	5	7	9	0.75	1.05	1.35
Frame quality	10	7	8	3	2.1	2.4
Brakes	4	6	5	0.4	0.6	0.5
Groupset	9	7	8	0.45	0.35	0.4
Total	34	35	37	7	7.3	7.45

Colnago C64 $7 \div (0.4 + 0.15 + 0.3 + 0.1 + 0.05) = 7$

Pinarello F10 = 7.3

De Rosa SK = 7.45

Steve should buy the De Rosa SK

Note that weightings add up to 1 as we are using percentages. This is not always the case.

Exercise 3G

Grade 8

1   Find the geometric mean of:
   a 4 and 16
   b 1.4 and 2.9
   c 3, 8 and 9
   d 2.5, 4.7 and 6.4
   e 3, 6, 8 and 11
   f 2, 5, 13, 17 and 24.

2   What would you multiply a sum of money (e.g. £60) by if you wanted to:
   a increase it by 4%
   b increase it by 3%
   c increase it by 12%
   d increase it by 2.5%
   e decrease it by 5%
   f decrease it by 13%?

3 Meghan invests some money for 5 years at 4% compound interest per year. By what percentage will the money have increased at the end of the five years?

4 On four consecutive days, the price of a share goes up by 4%, up by 2%, up by 5% and down by 3%. Use the geometric mean of the multipliers to find the average percentage change over the four days.

5 A new DJ takes over a popular radio programme. During the next month the listening figures go up by 15%, and in the following two months they rise by 6% and 3%. Use the geometric mean of the multipliers to find the average percentage change over the three months.   AO2

6 Nancy is investigating inflation between 2014 and 2018. This table gives the percentage increase in the price of a certain chocolate bar each year for five years: AO2

Year	2014	2015	2016	2017	2018
Percentage rise	12%	9%	7%	3%	5%

Use the geometric mean to find the average percentage rise.

7 Warm-air Ltd produce electric fan heaters.

During the last four years the cost of the heating element has changed. The following table shows these changes.   AO2

Year	Percentage price change
2014–2015	+14%
2015–2016	+5%
2016–2017	−3%
2017–2018	+7.5%

By what percentage has the heating element changed over this period?

8 Nancy finds this table, which shows how the price of a bottle of a certain drink has changed over time: AO2

Year	2014	2015	2016	2017	2018
Price	£1.10	£1.21	£1.28	£1.30	£1.35

The price in 2013 was exactly £1.

Work out the multipliers for each of the five years in the table and use the weighted mean to find the average percentage rise. Give your answer to one decimal place.

9 Using the weighted mean, the average percentage fall in the value of my car during the last two years was 28%.   AO2

If it fell 36% in the first year, by what percentage did it fall in the second year?

10 Michael writes down three numbers. He asks his friend Matthew to guess the numbers.   AO2

He tells Matthew that the mode of the numbers is 24 and the weighted mean is 12.

What are the three numbers?

11 Felicity is buying a new computer. She wants one with the following ratings: AO2

30% Speed

50% Screen quality

20% Hard drive type

The two models she is considering are rated out of 10 by a magazine as:

Dell: Speed 7 / Screen quality 10 / Hard drive 6

HP: Speed 6 / Screen quality 8 / Hard drive 10

Use a weighted average to decide on which machine Felicity should buy.

12 A Gymnastics competition uses a panel to judge gymnasts in a floor routine. **AO2**
The gymnasts are judged according to four criteria. Each judge is asked to
award a mark out of 10 for each criterion. Which gymnast wins the competition?

Area	Weighting (%)	Score out of 10		
		Kate	Bethan	Harriet
Difficulty	30	8	6	5
Execution	55	7	9	6
Artistic performance	10	5	7	7
Choreography	5	6	8	4
Overall score (out of 10)				

13 Milk is sold with different levels of fat: **AO2**

Skimmed: 1% fat

Semi-skimmed: 2% fat

Whole: 3.25% fat

A coffee shop only has skimmed and whole milk and wants to make 3 litres of semi-skimmed. How much of each type of milk needs to be mixed together to make the semi-skimmed milk?

3.8 Variance and standard deviation

Quick reminder

These two quantities measure spread: the more variation there is within a set of data, the bigger they will be.

e.g.   Set A consists of the six numbers   5, 5, 6, 6, 6, 7

   Set B consists of the six numbers   2, 4, 5, 6, 7, 9

The standard deviation and variance for Set B will be bigger than for Set A because the numbers in Set B are more spread out.

The formulae you should use for standard deviation are:

For a list of numbers: Standard deviation = $\sqrt{\dfrac{\Sigma x^2}{n} - \left(\dfrac{\Sigma x}{n}\right)^2}$ or $\sqrt{\dfrac{\Sigma x^2}{n} - (\bar{x})^2}$

For a frequency distribution: Standard deviation = $\sqrt{\dfrac{\Sigma fx^2}{\Sigma f} - \left(\dfrac{\Sigma x}{\Sigma f}\right)^2}$ or $\sqrt{\dfrac{\Sigma fx^2}{\Sigma f} - (\bar{x})^2}$

The variance has the same formulae but no square root signs, so:

For a list of numbers: $\qquad$ Variance $= \dfrac{\Sigma x^2}{n} - \left(\dfrac{\Sigma x}{n}\right)^2$ or $\dfrac{\Sigma x^2}{n} - (\overline{x})^2$

For a frequency distribution: $\quad$ Variance $= \dfrac{\Sigma fx^2}{f} - \left(\dfrac{\Sigma fx}{f}\right)^2$ or $\dfrac{\Sigma fx^2}{f} - (\overline{x})^2$

In each case, use the second version if you have already calculated the mean, $(\overline{x})^2$.

In the following exercise, you may use your calculator but you must write down enough working so that your method can be followed.

If your answers are not exact, round them to three significant figures.

Exercise 3H

Grade 6

1 Calculate the standard deviation for each of these sets of data:

a 3   7   8   10

b 2   5   9   12   13   16   17   20

c 1.7   2.3   2.9   3.4   5.6   6.8   9.5   10.1   12.3   13.4

2 Jane's exam marks last summer were:

67   82   34   56   47   76   69   45   57

Calculate:

a her mean mark

b the standard deviation of her marks.

3 Calculate the standard deviation for the frequency tables below:

a

x	3	4	5	6
f	2	5	9	6

b

x	4	6	8	10	12
f	3	12	8	5	2

c

x	5	10	15	20	25	30
f	2	7	8	4	3	1

Grade 7

4 The table below shows the number of pets in 60 families:

Number of pets	0	1	2	3	4	5
Frequency	4	17	21	9	8	1

Calculate:

a the mean   **b** the variance   **c** the standard deviation.

5 The table below shows the number of televisions owned by 50 families:

Number of TVs	0	1	2	3	4	5
Number of families	6	7	14	17	5	1

Calculate:

a the mean   **b** the variance   **c** the standard deviation.

6 This table shows the number of books read this year by the 30 members of a reading group.

Number of books	Frequency
5	1
6	8
7	12
8	6
9	3

Calculate:

a the mean   **b** the variance.

7 The weights of 50 dogs (to the nearest kg) have been collected and put into this grouped frequency table.

Weight (kg)	Number of dogs
1–3	5
4–6	7
7–9	11
10–12	16
13–15	11

Using the mid-point of each class as x, calculate:

a an estimate of the mean

b an estimate of the variance.

8 Calculate an estimate of the standard deviation of each of these grouped frequency distributions, where x is a continuous variable:

a

Class	Frequency
$1 \leqslant x < 5$	2
$5 \leqslant x < 9$	4
$9 \leqslant x < 13$	5
$13 \leqslant x < 17$	3
$17 \leqslant x \leqslant 21$	1

b

Class	Frequency
$10 \leqslant x < 20$	7
$20 \leqslant x < 30$	9
$30 \leqslant x < 40$	4
$40 \leqslant x < 50$	2
$50 \leqslant x \leqslant 60$	2

c

Class	Frequency
$0 \leqslant x < 5$	15
$5 \leqslant x < 10$	7
$10 \leqslant x < 15$	4
$15 \leqslant x < 20$	3
$20 \leqslant x \leqslant 25$	2

9 The heights of 80 seedlings have been measured correct to the nearest cm and the results put in this table.

Height (cm)	10–19	20–29	30–39	40–49	50–59	60–69	70–79
Number of seedlings	5	4	8	18	21	15	9

Calculate an estimate of the standard deviation.

10 For a set of data, $\Sigma f = 100$, $\Sigma fx = 347$ and $\Sigma fx^2 = 1942$.

Calculate the variance.

EQ 11 Stephanie recorded the time she took to travel to work on each of 50 days.

The table shows information about these times:

Time, x (minutes)	Frequency, f
$20 < x \leqslant 30$	4
$30 < x \leqslant 38$	9
$38 < x \leqslant 42$	12
$42 < x \leqslant 50$	18
$50 < x \leqslant 60$	7

a Calculate an estimate of the mean time Stephanie took to travel to work.

b Calculate an estimate of the standard deviation of these times.

You may use $\Sigma fx^2 = 91\,367$.

c Interpret your answer to part **b**.　　　　　　　　　　　　　　　　　　AO2

Grade 8

12 Jada can sell all of the pumpkins grown on his farm to a supermarket, as long　　AO2
as 85% of them weigh between 750 g and 1.5 kg.

Weight, w (g)	$500 \leqslant w < 750$	$750 \leqslant w < 1000$	$1000 \leqslant w < 1250$	$1250 \leqslant w < 1500$	$1500 \leqslant w < 1750$
Frequency	22	63	98	53	7

Will the supermarket accept Jada's pumpkins?

3.9 Box plots, outliers and skewness

Box plots and outliers

Range = largest value − smallest value

For *n* values:

Lower quartile Q1 = 1/4(*n*+1)   Median Q2 = 1/2(*n*+1)   Upper quartile Q3 = 3/4(*n*+1)

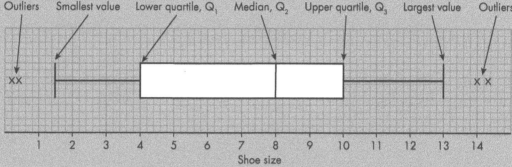

Outliers can be calculated using quartiles. An outlier is defined as an observation which is:

Less than Q1 − 1.5 (Q3 − Q1)   Greater than Q3 + 1.5 (Q3 − Q1)

Outliers are marked with an x as illustrated above.

Calculating skewness from a box plot

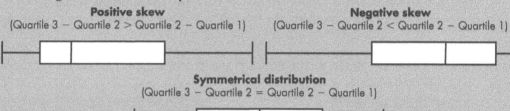

The mean, mode and median can be used to figure out if you have a positively or negatively skewed distribution.

Where mean > median > mode the distribution is positively skewed.

Where mean < median < mode, the distribution is negatively skewed.

The formula for calculating skewness is: $\textbf{Skew} = \dfrac{3(\textbf{mean} - \textbf{median})}{\textbf{standard deviation}}$

Exercise 3I

Grade 6

1   Draw a box plot for each set of the data in the table below.

	Smallest value	Lower quartile	Median	Upper quartile	Largest value
a	5	17	23	28	35
b	16	22	26	34	56
c	21	30	35	42	51

2 The box plot in the quick reminder shows the ages of a sample of 100 men.
A similar sample of 100 women was taken and the results were: youngest age = 24,
oldest age = 40, lower quartile = 27, median = 29, upper quartile = 34.

a Copy the diagram for the men and draw a box plot for the women using the same
scale above it.

b Comment on the difference between the two distributions, making reference   **AO2**
to the medians, the interquartile ranges and the skewness, and interpreting
the comparisons for someone who does not know what these statistics mean.

3 In a town there are two rival garages – Green's Garage and White's Garage. This box
plot shows the price of cars at Green's Garage.

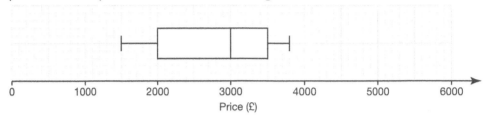

The same data for prices of cars at White's Garage is: cheapest car £2500, most
expensive £5000, lower quartile £3000, median £3300 and upper quartile £4000.

a Copy the diagram for Green's Garage and draw a box plot for White's Garage above it,
using the same scale.

b Comment on the differences between the two distributions, making   **AO2**
reference to the medians, the interquartile ranges and the skewness, and interpreting
the comparisons for someone who does not know what these statistics mean.

4 The table below shows the hours of sunshine each day recorded over a year in two
different resorts.

	Least hours	Lower quartile	Median	Upper quartile	Most hours
Resort A	5	7	9	11	13
Resort B	1	5	9	13	17

a Draw box plots to compare both sets of data.

b Comment on the differences between the distributions.   **AO2**

c Comment on the skewness of each box plot.

5 Hannah says that she expects the data she is going to collect about the pocket money   **AO2**
of Year 7 girls will be symmetrical. Do you think Hannah is correct? Explain your answer.

6 The table below shows the marks scored by 100 candidates in a maths exam.

Mark	No. of students
1–20	3
21–30	10
31–40	13
41–50	20
51–60	23
61–70	15
71–80	12
81–90	4

a Draw a cumulative frequency curve to show the data.

b Use your graph to estimate the median mark and the upper and lower quartiles.

c The lowest mark was 5 and the highest was 87. Draw a box plot to show the distribution of marks.

7 Nick has photocopied two box plots showing the September midday temperatures of Torrevieja and Granada, which are two towns in Spain.   **AO2**

Torrevieja is next to the sea. Granada is high in the mountains.

Unfortunately, the writing on the plots is not clear enough for Nick to read it.

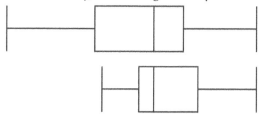

a Which box plot is the one for Granada? Explain your choice.

b Compare the midday temperatures shown by the two box plots.

c Comment on the skewness of each plot.

EQ **8** The box plot below shows the weights of 48 dogs as measured by a vet.   **AO2**

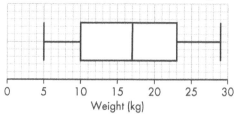

a Peter says the lightest dog is 10 kg. Explain why he is wrong.

b Write down the median weight.

c Calculate the interquartile range.

d How many dogs weighed 23 kg or more? Explain your answer.

9 The box plot shows the scores of 600 pupils who took a maths SAT exam.   **AO2**

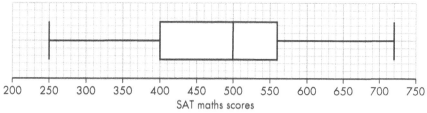

a Comment on the skewness of the graph. Support your answer with calculations.

b How many students scored between 400 and 500?

EQ **10** 27 track and field athletes each ran 200 metres. The time was recorded to the nearest second.

The stem-and-leaf diagram shows this information.

```
                    Athletes' times
    2 |  2  5  5  6  6  6  8  8  9
    3 |  1  2  3  3  3  4  6  6  7  7  7  8
    4 |  2  2  5  5  5
    5 |  5
```
Key: 3|1 = 31 seconds

a Use the information in the stem-and-leaf diagram to complete the following table.

Lowest value	
Lower quartile	28
Median	
Upper quartile	38
Highest value	

b Identify any outliers for the times of the athletes. Use calculations to justify your answer.   AO2

c On a grid, draw a box plot to show the distribution of the times of the athletes.

11 Here are four cumulative frequency curves and four box plots.   AO2

a Match each cumulative frequency curve with a box plot.

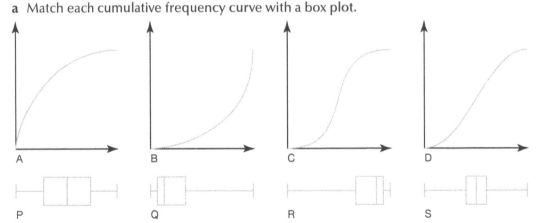

b Comment on the skewness of each graph.

12 A running club recorded the times taken by its members in a 10 km race.

The summary data is shown in the table.

Mean (min)	Standard deviation (min)	Median (min)
53.2	5.6	48.7

a Calculate the skewness of the data.

b Interpret your answer to **a** in context.   AO2

4 Scatter diagrams and correlation

4.1 Correlation and causal relationships

Quick reminder

A **scatter diagram** is a method of comparing two variables by plotting their corresponding values on a graph. These values are usually taken from a table. A **line of best fit** should be drawn through coordinates, representing the means of both variables.

There are different types of **correlation** – positive, negative and no correlation.

A **causal relationship** is when a change in one variable causes a change in another variable. For example, the size of a car engine and the amount of petrol the car uses, or sales of computers and sales of software. Sales of phones and sales of shoes is not a causal relationship.

Correlation can sometimes be confused with **causality**. If you are studying two variables X and Y and you change X, then there will be a change in Y if they are correlated. However, this does not mean that a change in X **causes** a change in Y.

Exercise 4A

Grade 4

 1 Data is to be collected from students for four pairs of variables.

    a For each pair of variables, will this data be positively correlated, negatively correlated or have no correlation? Give an explanation for each answer.

       i Shoe size and height

      ii Hair colour and number of friends

     iii Mathematics set and science set

     iv Hair colour and English set

    b Which of the variables i–iv are likely to have a causal relationship?

 2 Place the terms **positive correlation, no correlation** and **negative correction** into the blank spaces.

    a The number of ice-creams sold and the temperature are variables which are likely to show ....

    b The number of ice-creams sold and the amount of rainfall are variables which are likely to show ....

    c The number of people visiting a museum on different days and the number of copies of newspapers sold nationally are variables which are likely to show ....

3 Which of these variables are likely to have a causal relationship?

   a Alcohol consumption and reaction time

   b Hair colour and IQ

   c Road traffic accidents and driving conditions

   d Divorce rate and consumption of margarine

4 The heights and weights of 20 footballers are given in the table below.   AO2

Height	1.61	1.73	1.69	1.75	1.79	1.95	1.76	1.80	1.66	1.77
Weight	67	70	71	74	73	85	73	78	65	77
Height	1.78	1.82	1.91	1.75	1.77	1.82	1.86	1.85	1.65	1.68
Weight	74	83	87	70	72	77	75	77	72	68

   a Draw a scatter diagram to illustrate the data.

   b Calculate the mean of both data sets.

   c Draw a line of best fit on the graph.

   d David is a 1.7 m tall footballer. How heavy would you expect him to be?

5 A health clinic counted the number of breaths per minute and the number of   AO2
pulse beats per minute for 10 people doing various activities. This information is
shown in the table below.

Breaths per minute	16	20	20	24	26	28	28	30	34	36
Pulse beats per minute	58	68	70	72	84	80	84	88	94	102

   a Draw a scatter diagram to illustrate the data.

   b Calculate the mean of both data sets.

   c Draw a line of best fit on the graph.

   d Davila is breathing at a rate of 32 breaths per minute. Estimate her pulse beats per minute.

(EQ) **6** A researcher plotted the scatter diagram   AO2
opposite, which shows the relationship
between air temperature and elevation
above sea level.

   a What type of correlation does the scatter
diagram show?

   b Describe the relationship between air
temperature and elevation.

   c What is the height above sea level when
the air temp is 10 °C?

   d Comment on whether this is a causal
relationship.

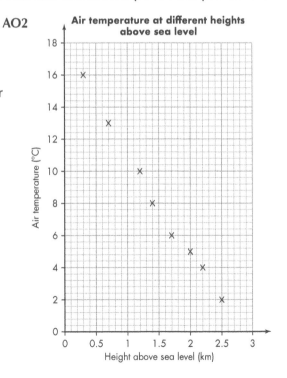

Air temperature at different heights above sea level

4.2 Interpolation, extrapolation and lines of regression

Quick reminder

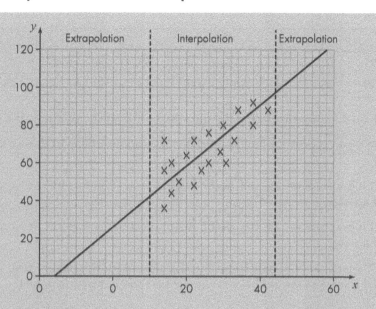

Interpolation is when you try to make an estimate from a scatter graph *inside* the data you have. It is always better to use interpolation, because it is more likely to be accurate.

Extrapolation is when you try to make an estimate from a scatter graph *outside* the data you have using the line of best fit. It is not always good to use, as you do not have the data for the area on the scatter graph that you are using, so you do not know (if at all) how accurate it will be.

Lines of regression are lines of best fit through a data set. They are given in the form of the equation of a straight line $y = mx + c$.

Exercise 4B

Grade 5

1   The table below shows the age and height of 10 gifted young basketball players.   **AO2**

Age (years)	11.9	12.4	12.8	13.7	14.4	15.2	15.8	15.9	16	16.4
Height (metres)	1.52	1.44	1.64	1.84	1.77	1.85	1.81	1.88	1.95	1.90

a   Plot the points on a scatter diagram.

b   Calculate the means of age and height and use these to draw a line of best fit.

c   Misca is a gifted basketball player who is 1.75 m tall. Estimate Misca's age.

d   Explain why it would not be sensible to extend the line of best fit so that you   **AO3**
     could determine the height of a 20-year-old basketball player.

2 The table below shows the test marks for 10 students in their English and history   AO2
tests.

Student	Ali	Brian	Clare	Dai	Ed	Farr	Greg	Henry	Ira	Jamir
English	35	61	62	27	34	59	66	45	82	39
History	36	35	54	25	30	55	60	45	75	65

   a Plot the data on a scatter diagram. Take the x-axis for English and the y-axis for history.

   b Calculate the mean scores for English and history and use these to draw a line of best fit.

   c One student felt unwell on the day of the English test. Who was this person? Explain your answer.

   d One student felt unwell on the day of the history test. Who was this person? Explain your answer.

   e Kali scored 70 marks in her English test but was absent for the history test. Estimate what score Kali would have got if she had taken the history test.

3 A tyre repair workshop has a faulty tyre pressure gauge.   AO2

   The gauge is checked against a correct gauge and the following data is obtained:

Reading of gauge (bar)	1.0	1.4	1.8	2.2	2.6	3.0	3.4	3.8
Correct reading (bar)	1.96	2.23	2.85	3.19	3.58	4.02	4.33	4.70

   a Plot the points on a scatter diagram.

   b Calculate the means both of the reading of the gauge and of the correct reading.

   c Draw a line of best fit on your graph.

   d Use your graph to work out the equation of the line in the form $y = mx + c$.

   e What is your interpretation of where the line crosses the y-axis?

4 The data from an experiment comparing reaction time for a simple task and   AO2
the blood/alcohol concentration (BAC) is given in the table below.

BAC (g/l)	0.01	0.02	0.05	0.08	0.10	0.12	0.18
Reaction time (seconds)	1.5	1.9	3.0	5.2	6.4	7.2	12.6

   a Plot the points on a graph.

   b Calculate the means of both blood/alcohol concentration and reaction time.

   c Draw a line of best fit on your graph.

   d Use your graph to work out the equation of the line in the form $y = mx + c$.

   e What is your interpretation of where the line crosses the y-axis?

5 The table below contains the exam marks of nine students in Maths and Physics.   **AO2**

Maths mark	23	37	32	79	46	68	90	81	62
Physics mark	41	39	34	76	61	86	87	95	51

a Draw a scatter diagram. Take the *x*-axis as maths mark.

b Calculate the means of both variables.

c Draw a line of best fit.

d Find the equation of your line of best fit in the form $y = mx + c$.

e Describe why this formula might not always be accurate.   **AO3**

6 A large supermarket records the number of customers (in thousands) and profit   **AO2**
(in thousands) for eight weeks.

Number of customers (1000s)	30	26	28	20	12	18	32	25
Profits (£000)	120	112	115	85	70	72	150	105

a Draw a scatter diagram. Take the *x*-axis as number of customers.

b Calculate the means of both variables.

c Draw a line of best fit.

d Find the equation of your line of best fit in the form $y = mx + c$.

e Describe why this formula might not always accurate.   **AO3**

7 The table below shows the hours of exercise per week and the resting heart   **AO2**
rates of eight people.

Total exercise per week (hrs)	7	3	5	11	10	12	2	6
Resting heart rate (bpm)	71	93	84	59	60	54	86	72

a Draw a scatter diagram. Take the *x*-axis as hours of exercise.

b Calculate the means of both variables.

c Draw a line of best fit.

d Find the equation of your line of best fit in the form $y = mx + c$.

e Describe why this formula might not always accurate.   **AO3**

4.3 Spearman's rank and Pearson product-moment correlation coefficients

Quick reminder

Both **Spearman's rank correlation coefficient (SRCC)** and the **Pearson product-moment correlation coefficient (PMCC)** are numerical measures of the correlation between two sets of data. They are used to find out if there is a relationship or connection between the data. For example, do students who do well in French exams also do well in English exams?

Both correlation coefficients range between –1 and +1 where –1 is perfect negative correlation and +1 is perfect positive correlation.

You are expected to be able to interpret both the SRCC and the PMCC in the context of a problem. However, you will only be asked to calculate the SRCC.

Spearman's rank correlation coefficient can be used when only rankings are given, e.g. two wine tasters putting 10 wines in order of preference.

It can also be used if you think there is a relationship which is nonlinear, e.g. a scatter graph showing a curve.

The Pearson product-moment correlation coefficient is used when a scatter graph shows an approximately **linear** relationship.

The formula to calculate Spearman's rank correlation coefficient is:

$$SRCC = 1 - \frac{6\Sigma d^2}{n(n^2-1)}$$

where n is the number of data values

Σd^2 is the sum of the squares of the differences between the ranks.

Exercise 4C

Grade 4

1 Michelle calculates Spearman's rank correlation coefficient for three different sets of data. Her results are shown in the table below.   AO2

Data sets	Spearman's rank correlation coefficient
a Hours of sunshine vs amount of rain	–0.92
b Size of diamond vs price of diamond	0.89
c Eye colour vs height	0.21

Comment on the relationship for each data set.

Grade 5

(EQ) 2 The following table shows the population and land area of eight European countries.

Country	Land area (km²)	Population (millions)	Land area rank	Population rank	d	d^2
Austria	83 871	8.21				
Belgium	30 528	10.42				
France	643 427	64.77				
Germany	357 022	82.28				
Luxemburg	2 586	0.49				
Ireland	70 273	4.62				
Spain	505 370	46.51				
UK	243 610	62.35				

a Copy and complete the table.

b Calculate Spearman's rank correlation coefficient for these data.

c Interpret your answer to part **b** in full.   AO2

Grade 6

3 Match the coefficients to the graphs.

a

b

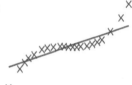

c

d

e

1 PMCC +1, SRCC +1

2 PMCC −1, SRCC −1

3 PMCC −0.8, SRCC −1

4 PMCC −0.01, SRCC −0.01

5 PMCC 0.87, SRCC +1

4 The table below shows the personal best times of 10 athletes for running 5000 m and 10 000 m in minutes and seconds.

Athlete	5000 m	10 000 m	5000 m rank	10 000 m rank	Difference d	d^2
A	15.36	31.34				
B	16.55	32.33				
C	13.50	30.02				
D	14.25	29.44				
E	17.32	38.23				
F	20.12	36.40				
G	14.48	29.57				
H	15.45	30.09				
I	14.58	28.52				
J	16.04	32.35				

a Copy and complete the table.

b Use the table to calculate Spearman's rank correlation coefficient.

c Comment on the relationship between the two sets of data. AO2

5 The table below shows the average daily rainfall and the average number of hours of sunshine at a weather station. AO2

Month	Rainfall (mm)	Sunshine (hours)	Rainfall rank	Sunshine rank	Difference d	d^2
January	1.36	1.2				
February	1.35	2.7				
March	0.75	4.6				
April	2.22	5.2				
May	2.54	5.7				
June	2.26	7.7				
July	2.99	5.2				
August	1.84	5.8				
September	2.66	4.9				
October	1.74	3.1				
November	1.57	2.9				
December	2.09	1.9				

a Copy and complete the table.

b Use the table to calculate Spearman's rank correlation coefficient.

c Comment on the relationship between the two sets of data.

6 Mr Meaner and Ms Take are judges at an art competition. The best 10 paintings are ranked by each of them. The results are in the table below:

Painting	A	B	C	D	E	F	G	H	I	J
Mr Meaner	5	3	10	5	7	8	1	2	9	4
Ms Take	8	1	9	7	4	5	3	2	10	6

a Use the table to calculate Spearman's rank correlation coefficient.

b Comment on how well (or not) the two judges agree.   AO2

7 For the graph below, which correlation measure would you use? Explain your answer.

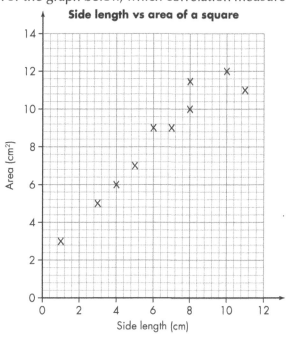

Side length vs area of a square

Grade 8

8 Alicia thinks that her friends who are good at Spanish are also good at German.   AO2
Is she correct?

Name	Zola	Yves	Xavier	Will	Viki	Uri	Toni	Sal	Rico	Qamra
Spanish exam result	9	12	16	12	10	7	12	12	8	16
German exam result	10	10	13	8	6	4	7	6	5	7

9 Using anonymous data from her local hospital, Lily draws up the following table: AO2

Patient	A	B	C	D	E	F	G	H	I	J
Number of years smoking	12	23	24	28	30	33	37	42	43	47
Percentage damage to lungs	18	52	55	28	59	41	59	66	61	69

Lily thinks that the longer a person smokes, the worse their lung damage is likely to be. Is she correct?

4.3 Spearman's rank and Pearson product-moment correlation coefficients

5 Time series

5.1 Moving averages

Quick reminder

Time series analysis shows how the values of data change over time and can be used to identify patterns in the data. It can also be used to show underlying trends and seasonal variation.

Moving averages are used to smooth out seasonal variation and are calculated by grouping data, in sequence, depending upon the type of moving average that is required. For example, a 3-point moving average would be obtained from the mean of the first three items of data, then the second to fourth items, and so on. A 4-point moving average takes the data in groups of four.

Seasonal variation = actual value – trendline value

$$\text{Mean seasonal variation} = \frac{\Sigma(\text{actual value} - \text{trendline value})}{\text{total number of quarters}}$$

Estimated seasonal variation = value from trend line + mean seasonal variation at that point (e.g. Quarter 3 mean)

Exercise 5A

Grade 2

1. This line graph shows the outside temperature at a weather station, taken at four-hour intervals during one day. **AO2**

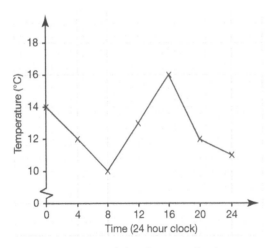

a At what time of the day was the lowest temperature?

b What was the highest temperature?

c Between which two readings was the greatest temperature change?

d Estimate the temperature at 10 am.

e When the outside temperature at the weather station goes above 13°C, the heating stops inside the building. For how long does the heating stop on this day?

Grade 4

2 Jon goes to a pub quiz once a week for eight weeks. The table shows his scores.   AO2

Week	1	2	3	4	5	6	7	8
Score (out of 100)	35	47	54		68	74	78	82

a Draw a line graph for the data.

b Jon could not remember his score on the fourth week. Use your graph to estimate Jon's score on the fourth week.

c Explain the trend in Jon's scores. What reasons can you give to explain this trend?

d Explain why it would be a mistake to use your graph to estimate Jon's score   AO3
in the 12th week of the pub quiz.

3 The table shows how much tourists spent in the UK between 1998 and 2018.   AO2

Total spending (£ billions)	6.2	7.9	12.3	12.8	13.0	16.3
Year	1998	2002	2006	2010	2014	2018

a Draw a line graph for the data.

b Use your graph to estimate tourist spending in 2022.

c Explain the trend in tourist spending. What reasons can you give to explain this trend?

d Explain why many people think that tourist spending in 2022 will be much higher than your answer to part **b**.

4 The time series graph shows information about the average number of barn   AO2
owl eggs hatched in different parts of a large protection area from 2007 to 2015.

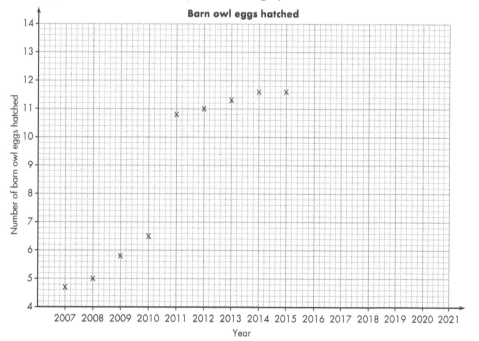

a Explain what the time series graph shows you about the average number of barn owl eggs that hatched in the protection area from 2007 to 2015.

b Use the information in the time series graph from 2011 to 2015 to predict the number of barn owl eggs that will hatch in 2021.

c Comment on the reliability of your prediction. AO3

Grade 5

5 The table shows the number of goldfish born in a large garden pond from 2003 to 2010.

Year	2011	2012	2013	2014	2015	2016	2017	2018
No. of goldfish born	66	68	60	51	44	36	30	25

a Plot a graph from the data in the table and draw a trend line for it.

b Use your graph to estimate the likely number of goldfish that will be born in 2019.

c Between which two years did the number of goldfish born decrease the most?

d What reasons can you give to explain this trend?

e Is it possible to use this data to predict the likely number of goldfish born in 2028? AO3

6 The table shows the average price of a two-bedroom flat at certain distances from the seafront of a popular seaside town. AO3

Distance from seafront (km)	0	1	2	3	4
Average price (£ thousands)	250	180	175	169	164

a Plot a graph from the data in the table and draw a trend line for it.

b Use your graph to estimate the average price of a two-bedroom flat 5 km from the seafront. AO2

c What reasons can you give to explain this trend?

d Is it possible to use this data to predict the average price of a two-bedroom flat 10 km from the seafront? Explain your answer. AO3

Grade 6

7 This table shows the cost of a household's gas consumption over a three-year period.

Year	2016				2017				2018			
Quarter	Q1	Q2	Q3	Q4	Q1	Q2	Q3	Q4	Q1	Q2	Q3	Q4
Cost (£)	134	78	52	120	144	76	59	133	158	84	60	
4-point moving average		96	98.50	98	99.75	103						

a Show that the first 4-point moving average is £96.

b Calculate the last three 4-point moving averages.

c Copy the graph below and plot the last three moving averages.

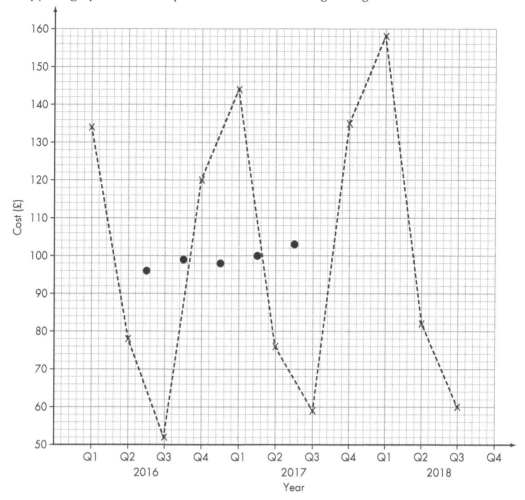

d Use your trend line to calculate the mean seasonal effect in the 4th quarter.

e Use the mean seasonal effect to calculate the 4th quarter of 2018

Grade 7

EQ 8 A calculator manufacturer shows the following quarterly (Q), or three-monthly, sales figures (in thousands).

AO2

Quarterly sales figures in 1000s			
	Q1	Q2	Q3	Q4
2017	42	46	40	42
2018	44	48	42	46

a Calculate the 4-point moving averages for these data.

b Plot a graph showing the sales figures and the 4-point moving averages.

c Describe and interpret the trends seen in the sales of their calculators.

9 The information below shows a household's electricity bill over a three-year period.

Year	Period	Electricity bill (£)
1	Jan–Apr	95
	May–Aug	63
	Sept–Dec	150
2	Jan–Apr	110
	May–Aug	71
	Sept–Dec	175
3	Jan–Apr	120
	May–Aug	76
	Sept–Dec	205

   a Use a 3-point moving average to draw a trendline.

   b Calculate the mean seasonal variation in May–Aug.

EQ **10** This time-series graph shows information about the quarterly electricity bills paid by a household from 2015 to 2017.

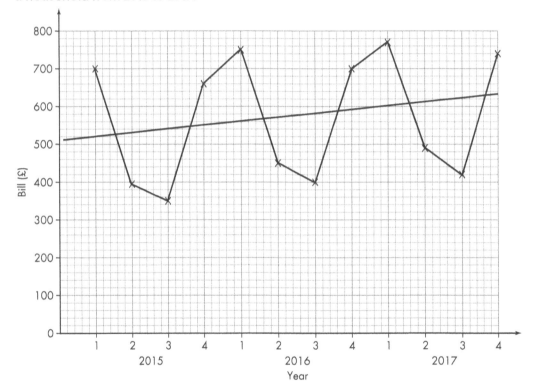

   a Calculate the mean seasonal variation for Quarter 3.

   b Calculate the mean seasonal variation for Quarter 1 and use it to estimate the household's bill in the first quarter of 2018.   **AO2**

   c Write down two assumptions you have made in part **b** that affect the validity of your answer.   **AO3**

11 The table gives information about the number of students opting for a Statistics module at a university over a three-year period.

Year	Term	Number of students	3-point moving average
1	Autumn	325	
	Spring	178	
	Summer	89	
2	Autumn	389	
	Spring	234	
	Summer	160	
3	Autumn	434	
	Spring	267	
	Summer	199	

a Complete the table.

b Draw a time series graph of the data.

c Plot the 3-point moving averages on the graph.

d Using your graph, calculate an estimate of the mean seasonal variation in the summer term. AO2

12 The table shows the number of iPhones sold by a high-street shop in each of the first five months of 2018.

Month	January	February	March	April	May
Number of iPhones	3170	3219	3290	3370	3590

a Work out the 3-point moving averages for the first five months of 2018.

b The 3-point moving average of the numbers of iPhones sold in December, January and February was 3210. Calculate the number of iPhones sold in December 2017.

6 Probability

6.1 Probability scale

Quick reminder

Probability is the chance or likelihood that something will happen. All probabilities lie between 0 and 1.

A probability of 0 means it is **impossible** for the event to happen.

A probability of 1 means the event is **certain** to happen.

Exercise 6A

Grade 1

1 Match each of these words to each statement.

impossible   certain   even chance   likely   unlikely

a I will wake up in the morning with seven heads.

b I will get tails when I throw a fair coin.

c I will be older next week than I am today.

d I will watch television this week.

e I will have no homework during a school week.

Grade 2

2 A fair four-sided spinner is numbered 1, 1, 2, 3.

The spinner is spun once.

Copy the probability scale. Put an arrow on the scale to show the probability of each of these outcomes.

```
0            0.5           1
```

a The spinner lands on a 1. Label this A.

b The spinner lands on a number greater than zero. Label this B.

c The spinner lands on an odd number. Label this C.

6.2 Equally likely outcomes

Quick reminder

The possible results of a trial are called **outcomes**.

The probability of an event happening $= \dfrac{\text{number of successful outcomes}}{\text{total number of possible outcomes}}$

This is known as **theoretical probability**.

The probability of an event **not** happening is 1 – the probability of the event happening.

Exercise 6B

Grade 3

1. A bag contains three red balls, four blue balls and six green balls. If a ball is chosen at random from the bag, what is the probability that it is:
   a a red ball
   b a green ball
   c a yellow ball
   d a blue or red ball?

2. A box contains 21 counters: 7 are red, 4 are blue and the rest are green. If a counter is taken at random from the box, what is the probability that it is:
   a red
   b green
   c red or green?

3. A card is drawn at random from a full pack of 52 playing cards. What is:
   a P(four of Hearts)
   b P(a Club)
   c P(a black card)
   d P(a Queen)
   e P(not a Queen)?

4. In a raffle, 1000 tickets are sold. Amy buys 12 tickets, Ruby buys 3 tickets, Colin buys 20 tickets and Rebecca buys 6 tickets. If there is only one winning ticket, what is the probability that:
   a Ruby wins
   b Colin wins
   c one of the girls wins
   d Amy will not win?

5. The probability of picking an ace from a pack of cards is $\frac{1}{13}$.
   What is the probability of **not** picking an ace from a pack of cards?

6. The probability that Sarah sends a text on any given day is 0.72.
   Work out the probability that Sarah does **not** send a text on any given day.

6.3 Expectation

Quick reminder

When you know the probability of an event, you can predict how many times that you would expect the event to happen. This is called **expectation**.

Grade 5

1 The probability that Sarah sends a text on any given day is 0.7. Work out how many texts (to the nearest whole number) that you would expect Sarah to send in one week (7 days).

EQ **2** A five-sided spinner is biased and has these probabilities of landing on each face.

Number	1	2	3	4	5
Probability	0.2	0.1	0.3	0.25	

a Explain how the table shows that the spinner is biased.

b What is the probability that it lands on 5?

c I spin the spinner 200 times, how many times might I expect it to land on 3?

EQ **3** A school snack bar offers a choice of four snacks: fish, pizza, pasta and chicken.

Students can choose **one** of these four snacks.

The table shows the probability that a student will choose burger or pizza or chicken.

Snack	Fish	Pizza	Pasta	Chicken
Probability	0.25	0.35		0.1

a 600 students used the snack bar on Wednesday. Work out an estimate for the number of students who chose pasta.

b The choice of snacks are mutually exclusive. Explain how you have used this to work out your answer in part **a**.

EQ **4** A bag contains some yellow balls, some blue balls, some green balls and some pink balls.

William is going to take one ball at random from the bag.

The table shows the probabilities that the ball will be yellow, blue or pink.

Colour	Yellow	Blue	Green	Pink
Probability	0.34	0.17		0.28

a Explain why the colours of the ball chosen are mutually exclusive.

b William repeats the experiment 200 times, replacing the ball each time. Work out an estimate for the number of green balls William selected.

5 Alex buys five raffle tickets. She is told that her probability of winning is $\frac{1}{125}$. How many tickets are there in the raffle altogether?

6 If I roll two fair normal dice 500 times, on how many occasions would I expect to score a total of 5 or less?   **AO2**

6.4 Experimental probability

Quick reminder

In real-life situations, the probabilities of different outcomes are not always equal or possible to work out. In such cases an experiment will need to be carried out. This gives the experimental probability or **relative frequency**. The relative frequency of an event is an estimate for the theoretical probability.

Relative frequency of an outcome or event = $\dfrac{\text{the number of successful outcomes}}{\text{the total number of trials}}$

Exercise 6D

Grade 4

1. You can find probabilities by: AO3

   A looking at historical data

   B using equally likely outcomes

   C using a survey or experiment.

   Which method would you use to find the probability that:

   a when a dice is rolled, the number will be a 1

   b Adrian would be good at taking penalty kicks

   c Sam will be late to school some time next week

   d a three-sided spinner is fair?

Grade 5

2. Thomas throws a fair six-sided dice and records how many times he gets a two.

   After 50 throws, he has scored 4 twos.

   After 100 throws, he has scored 9 twos.

   After 150 throws, he has scored 16 twos.

   After 200 throws, he has scored 21 twos.

   After 600 throws, he has scored 91 twos.

   After 1000 throws, he has scored 168 twos.

   After 2000 throws, he has scored 331 twos.

   a What is the theoretical probability of throwing a two with a dice?

   b Calculate the experimental probability of scoring a two after:

i 50 throws	v 600 throws
ii 100 throws	vi 1000 throws
iii 150 throws	vii 2000 throws
iv 200 throws.	

   c If Thomas threw the dice 12 000 times, how many twos would you expect him to get?

3 Jessica carries out an experiment to work out the probability that when she drops a drawing pin, it will land point up.

The table shows her results after 100, 200, 500, 1000, 1500, 2000, 2500 and 3000 trials.

Number of times pin is dropped	100	200	500	1000	1500	2000	2500	3000
Number of times pin lands point up	87	148	335	584	883	1182	1492	1797

a Calculate the experimental probability of a drawing pin landing point up after

   i   100 trials   **v**   1500 trials

   ii   200 trials   **vi**   2000 trials

   iii 500 trials   **vii** 2500 trials

   iv 1000 trials   **viii** 3000 trials.

b What do you think the experimental probability of the drawing pin landing point up is?

c If 18 000 of these drawing pins were dropped, how many would you expect to land points up?

4 Verity works in a factory making chips for computers. One of her jobs is to test a sample each day to make sure they work properly.   **AO2**

	Monday	Tuesday	Wednesday	Thursday	Friday
Number tested	910	670	1250	887	526
Number faulty	13	9	19	11	5

On which day is it most likely that the highest number of faulty computer chips were produced?

5 400 drivers in Manchester were asked if they had ever gone down a road with a 'No Entry' sign. 27 answered that they had.   **AO2**

There are 148 000 drivers in Manchester. How many of these do you estimate will have gone down a road with a 'No Entry' sign?

6 Rupinder spun this spinner 300 times.   **AO2**

She said, 'If this is a fair spinner I will get 100 number 4s.'

Explain why she is wrong.

7 Jason takes his young son Aaron to a 'ball pool'.   **AO2**

A sign says there are 500 000 coloured balls in the pool.

Aaron throws balls to Jason at random. Jason notes their colours and throws them back.

Colour	Red	Blue	Yellow	Green
Frequency	37	19	29	15

Work out how many red balls there are likely to be in the ball pool.

8 Samuel throws a six-sided dice 120 times with these results.

Number on dice	1	2	3	4	5	6
Frequency	17	19	11	33	22	18

   a Why might Samuel think that the dice is biased?   **AO2**

   b What could Samuel do to make his results more reliable?   **AO3**

EQ **9** Kuschal and Emily are testing a spinner to see if it is fair. The spinner has four equal sections: one is blue, one is green, one is black and one is red.

Kuschal spins the spinner 20 times. It lands on black 4 times.

   a What is the relative frequency of it landing on black after these 20 spins?

   b Emily spins the spinner 100 times. It lands on black 23 times. Explain why Emily's   **AO3**
results should be more reliable than Kuschal's results.

   c Combine Kuschal's data and Emily's data to estimate the probability that this spinner lands on black.

10 Which of these would suggest bias?

   a Getting a tail 2 times when flipping a coin 15 times.

   b Getting 23 ones on a four-sided spinner labelled 1 to 4, in 100 spins.

   c Getting 3 fives when rolling a dice 60 times.

6.5 Sample space diagrams

When two events happen at the same time, all possible outcomes can be shown in a **sample space diagram**. One event is written in the rows of the table and one event is written in the columns of the table.

Exercise 6E

Grade 4

1 A coin and fair six-sided dice are thrown. The sample space diagram shows the possible outcomes.

		Dice					
		1	2	3	4	5	6
Coin	Head	(H, 1)	(H, 2)	(H, 3)	(H, 4)	(H, 5)	(H, 6)
	Tail	(T, 1)	(T, 2)	(T, 3)	(T, 4)	(T, 5)	(T, 6)

What is the probability of getting a tail and a two?

EQ **2** Two four-sided spinners are used in a game. The first spinner is labelled 2, 4, 6, 8   **AO2**
and the second spinner is labelled 3, 5, 5, 7.

Both spinners are spun and their scores added together.

This sample space diagram shows all the ways the two
spinners can land.

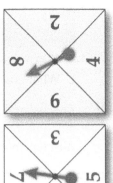

		Spinner 1			
		2	4	6	8
Spinner 2	3				
	5				
	5				
	7				

a Copy and complete the table to show the total scores.

b Jess says it is impossible for the total score to be an even
number. Is Jess correct? Explain your answer.

c What is the most likely total score? Give the probability of this score.

d What is the probability of getting a total score of 7 or 13?

Grade 5

EQ **3** Two fair dice are used in a game.

Both dice are thrown and their scores are **multiplied** together.

a Draw a sample space diagram to show the total scores.

b When the two dice are thrown together, what is the probability that the total score
will be:

   i a score of 7   **ii** a score of 12   **iii** a multiple of 5?

c Jack and Jill are playing a game with the spinners. Jack wins a point if the product
of the scores is even and Jill wins a point if the product is odd. Is the game fair?
Justify your answer.

4 There are two spinners: one with three sides numbered 2, 3, and 4 and the other with
eight sides numbered 1, 2, 3, 4, 5, 6, 7 and 8. The two spinners are spun and their
scores are added together. What is the probability that the sum is:

   a 7   **b** odd   **c** less than 6?

5 A three-sided spinner numbered 2, 2 and 3 and a four-sided dice, numbered 1, 2,
3 and 4 are thrown. The two scores are **multiplied** together.

What is:

a P(2)   **d** **i** Which is the most likely score?

b P(9)   **ii** What is the probability of that score?

c P(10)?

6 Alice, Beth, Craig and Daniel are playing in a squash competition. Each player in   **AO2**
the competition plays every other player. There are six matches altogether.
Two players are picked at random to play the first game. Work out the probability
that the first game will be played by a male player and a female player.

7 Hal is playing a game with two fair spinners.

He wins if both spinners land on 'Win'.

What is the probability of Hal winning?

AO2

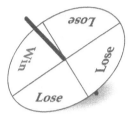 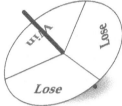

8 Ishmael makes this game to raise money for charity.

Contestants pay £1 to play.

They roll two fair 10-sided dice, each numbered from 1 to 10.

If they score a 5 on one dice, they win £1.

If they score a total of 5, they win £2.

If they score a double 5, they win £10.

Is he likely to make or lose money for the charity?

AO2

6.6 Venn diagrams

Venn diagrams consist of circles that may overlap. These represent sets. In maths a set is a collection of items or numbers. You can place these items in a Venn diagram to help you to calculate probabilities.

A set of numbers = {1, 2, 3, 4, 5, 6, 7, 8, 9, 10, 11, 12, 13, 14, 15, 16}

Set A = {multiples of 3}

Set B = {multiples of 5}

You place these items in the Venn diagam as shown.

Note:

Elements 3,6,9,12 are only in Set A.

Elements 5,10 are only in Set B.

Element 15 is in both sets.

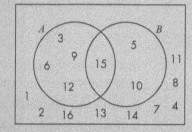

Elements 1,2,4,7,8,11,13,14,16 are not in Set A or B so are placed in the rectangle.

Using set notation

A intersection B $A \cap B = \{15\}$

A union B $A \cup B = \{3,5,6,9,10,12,15\}$

Note: 15 appears twice as it is in both sets.

Probabilities

Using the information in the Venn diagram:

$P(A) = \dfrac{5}{16}$ $\qquad$ $P(A \cap B) = \dfrac{1}{16}$

$P(B) = \dfrac{3}{16}$ $\qquad$ $P(A \cup B) = \dfrac{7}{16}$

Exercise 6F

Grade 3

 1 There are 50 students in Year 10.

    9 students study French and Spanish.

    15 students only study French.

    5 students do not study French or Spanish.

  a Draw a Venn diagram to show this information.

  b How many students only study Spanish?

 2 The Venn diagram below shows the choices made by people attending fitness   **AO2** sessions at a Gym.

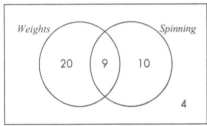

  a How many people chose weights and spinning?

  b How many people only chose weights?

  c How many people chose something other than weights or spinning?

Grade 5

 3 In a class of 32 pupils, 8 pupils play the drums, 15 pupils play the guitar and 12 pupils play neither instrument.

  a Show this information on a Venn diagram.

  b How many pupils play drums and guitar?   **AO2**

  c How many pupils only play the guitar?

  d A pupil is selected at random. What is the probability that they only play the drums?

 4 In an Academy school there are 90 teachers.

    35 teachers drink tea.

    54 teachers drink coffee.

    14 teachers drink neither.

  a Draw a Venn diagram to represent this information.

  b A teacher is selected at random. What is the probability they drink both tea   **AO2** and coffee?

5 The Venn diagram below shows the probability of events A and B happening.   AO2

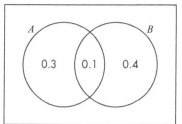

   a Complete the Venn diagram.

   b Write down $P(A \cap B)$.

   c Write down $P(A \cup B)$.

Grade 7

6 The Venn diagram below represents the types of pets owned by 80 primary   AO2
school pupils.

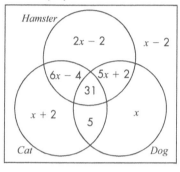

   a Form an equation in x and solve it.

   b How many pupils only own a dog?

   c How many pupils do not own a pet?

   d A pupil is selected at random. Write down the probability that they own a hamster and a dog but not a cat.

7 45 pupils study sciences at Henry Tudor School. All pupils study at least one science.

     34 study biology.

     16 study chemistry.

     5 do not study biology or chemistry.

     2 study biology chemistry and physics.

     4 study biology and physics but not chemistry.

     2 study only chemistry.

   a Draw a Venn diagram to represent this information.

   b A pupil is selected at random. What is the probability that they will only be   AO2
studying biology and chemistry?

   c How many pupils study physics?

6.7 Mutually exclusive events

Quick reminder

Mutually exclusive events are events that cannot happen at the same time, for example throwing an even number on a dice and throwing an odd number on a dice. Since there are no other possibilities, they are also called exhaustive events.

For mutually exclusive events: $P(A \text{ or } B) = P(A) + P(B)$

For events that are not mutually exclusive: $P(A \text{ or } B) = P(A) + P(B) - P(A \text{ and } B)$

This is illustrated below in Venn diagram format.

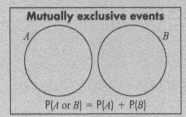

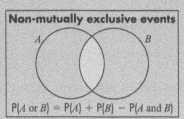

Exercise 6G

Grade 4

1 A box of chocolates contains 13 chocolates which look identical from the outside. Five of the chocolates have toffee centres, seven have soft centres and one has a nut centre.

One chocolate is taken at random from the box.

What is the probability that the chocolate:

a has a soft centre

b has a nut centre

c has a toffee or nut centre

d has a soft or toffee centre

e does not have a soft centre?

EQ 2 A bag contains three red beads, four blue beads and five green beads. A bead is taken from the bag at random. What is the probability of choosing:

a a green bead

b a blue bead

c a green or red bead

d a red, blue or green bead?

e Explain why your answer to **d** shows that selecting a red bead, selecting a blue   **AO2** bead and selecting a green bead are mutually exclusive events.

3 A letter is chosen at random from the word STATISTICS. What is the probability that it is:

a the letter S

b the letter I

c the letter A or T

d a vowel

e the letters S, A or T?

Grade 5

4 Libby takes a card at random from a full pack of 52 playing cards. What is:

 a P(3 of Spades)   **d** P(a Heart or the 3 of Spades)

 b P(a black card)   **e** P(a red card or the 3 of Spades)?

 c P(a Heart)

5 James has a set of 11 cards numbered from 1 to 11.

 He picks out a card and then replaces it in the pack.

 What is the probability that the number on the card is:

 a a multiple of 3   **c** an even number greater than 4

 b an odd number   **d** an odd number or an even number greater than 4?

6 Sarah, Lucy and Josh are playing a card game. The probability that Sarah wins is 0.3 and the probability that Josh wins is 0.25. Who is more likely to win the game?

7 Rob, Jack and Will are playing darts. The probability that Rob wins is $\frac{2}{7}$. The probability that either Rob or Will win is $\frac{3}{5}$. Which of the three players is most likely to win?

8 Broughton, the famous pub quizzer, has a random question generator   **AO2**
on his iPad. It contains 16 000 pub-quiz questions.

 It has four basic categories: 'science and nature', 'history and geography', 'literature, art and music' and 'weird stuff'.

 The probability of a 'history and geography' or a 'literature, art and music' question coming up is 0.55.

 The probability of a 'history and geography' or a 'science and nature' question coming up is 0.65.

 The probability of a 'literature, art and music' question **not** coming up is 0.7.

 Use this information to copy and complete the table below:

Type	Probability	Number of questions
Science and nature		
History and geography		
Literature, art and music		
Weird stuff		

Grade 6

9 P(A) = 0.5   **AO2**
P(B) = 0.8
P(A or B) = 0.7

 a Find P(A and B).

 b Are events A and B mutually exclusive?

10 X is the probability that a person has blue eyes. P(X) = 0.2.   **AO2**

Y is the probability that a person has brown hair. P(Y) = 0.7.

The probability that a person has blue eyes and brown hair. P(X and Y) = 0.1.

a Calculate P(X or Y). Describe this event.

b What is the probability that a randomly selected person has neither blue eyes nor brown hair?

11 A survey of students shows that 40% own a smartphone, 70% own a smart watch and 30% own both.

A student is chosen at random

a What is the probability they own a smartphone or a smart watch?   **AO2**

b What is the probability they own neither?

6.8 Independent events

Two events are said to be independent if the outcome of one does not affect the other.

For independent events A and B:

$P(A \text{ and } B) = P(A) \times P(B)$

Exercise 6H

Grade 3

1 Which of the following events are independent?   **AO2**

a Throwing a 3 with one die and a 5 with another.

b Picking an 8 from a deck of cards, keeping it, and picking a King.

c Flipping a tail with a coin and rolling a 9 with a die.

d Drawing a club and drawing a heart from the same deck without replacing the first card.

2 A and B are independent events. P(A) = 0.3, P(B) = 0.6.

Work out P(A and B).

3 A and B are independent events. P(A) = 0.4, P(A and B) = 0.32.

Calculate P(B).

Grade 4

4 A jar contains three red, five green, two blue and six yellow marbles. A marble is   **AO2**
chosen at random from the jar. After replacing it, a second marble is chosen.

a What is the probability of choosing a blue and then a yellow marble?

b What is the probability of choosing a green and then a red marble?

5 A card is chosen at random from a deck of 52 cards. It is then replaced and a second card is chosen.

    a What is the probability of choosing a 7 and then a Queen?   **AO2**

    b Why are these independent events?   **AO3**

6 A school survey found that 6 out of 10 pupils like beans and chips for lunch.   **AO2**
Three pupils are chosen at random. What is the probability that all three pupils like beans and chips?

7 The probability that James has chicken wings for dinner is 0.7. The probability   **AO2**
that his bike will suffer a puncture on the way to university is 0.2. These events are independent.

Calculate:

    a the probability that James will have chicken wings and a puncture

    b the probability that he will not have chicken wings for dinner

    c the probability that he will not have chicken wings or a puncture.

8 A letter is chosen at random from the alphabet and replaced. A second letter is   **AO2**
then chosen.

Find the probability that:

    a both are vowels

    b both are consonants

    c one is a vowel and one is a consonant.

9 The probability that Arabella will walk to school is 0.1. The probability she   **AO2**
will eat breakfast before leaving is 0.4 and the probability she will forget her lunch is 0.6. These events are independent.

    a What is the probability that she will forget her lunch, walk to school and eat breakfast?

    b What is the probability that she will walk to school, forget her lunch and not have breakfast?

    c What is the probability that she doesn't walk to school, doesn't eat breakfast and remembers to take her lunch?

6.9 Tree diagrams

Quick reminder

Tree diagrams are useful when working out the probability of combined events.

Exercise 6I

Grade 6

1 Bina has two fair four-sided spinners: Spinner A and Spinner B.

Spinner A

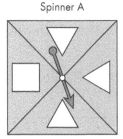

Spinner B

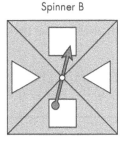

On Spinner A there are three triangles and one square, and on Spinner B there are two triangles and two squares.

Bina spins each spinner once.

Copy and complete the tree diagram to show the probabilities when each spinner is spun.

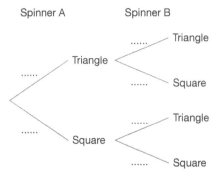

a What is the probability that both spinners land on triangles?

b What is the probability that one of the spinners lands on a triangle and the other spinner lands on a square?

Bina says that for each spinner getting a triangle and getting a square are mutually exclusive events.

c Explain why Bina is correct. AO2

2 Chloe throws a fair red dice once and a fair green dice once.

a Copy and complete the probability tree diagram to show the outcomes. Label clearly the branches of the probability tree diagram.

The probability tree diagram has been started in the space below:

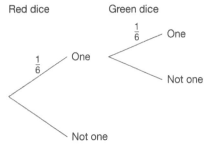

b What is the probability that both spinners land on a one? AO2

c What is the probability that only one of the spinners lands on a one?

3 Jonathan plays one game of tennis and one game of darts.

The probability that Jonathan will win at tennis is $\frac{4}{7}$.

The probability that Jonathan will win at darts is $\frac{1}{3}$.

a Copy and complete the probability tree diagram.

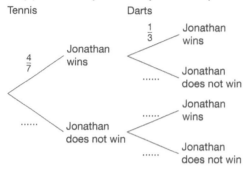

b Work out the probability that Jonathan wins both games.   **AO2**

c Work out the probability that Jonathan wins just one game.

4 The probability that Matthew is late for school on any particular day is 0.4.
The probability that Daisy is late for school on any particular day is 0.65.

The probabilities of Matthew and Daisy being late for school are independent.

a Copy and complete the probability tree diagram.

Matthew   Daisy

                    0.65 — Late
        Late <
    0.4   Not late

                    Late
    ...... Not late <
                    Not late

b Work out the probability that both Matthew and Daisy will be late for   **AO2**
school on any particular day.

c Work out the probability that Matthew will be late and Daisy will not be late for
school on any particular day.

d Work out the probability that either Matthew or Daisy will be late for school on
any particular day.

5 Ben travels to work on a bus and a train. The probability that the bus is on time is 0.7. The
probability that the train is on time is 0.6. Both events are independent of each other.

a Copy and complete the probability tree diagram.

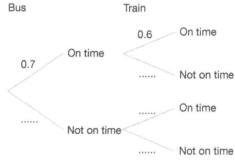

b Work out the probability that both the bus and the train are on time. **AO2**

c Work out the probability that the bus is on time and the train is late.

d Work out the probability that both the bus and the train are late.

6 Mr Smith and Mrs Tate both go to the library every Wednesday. The probability that Mr Smith takes out a fiction book is 0.8. The probability that Mrs Tate takes out a fiction book is 0.4. The events are independent.

a Copy and complete the probability tree diagram.

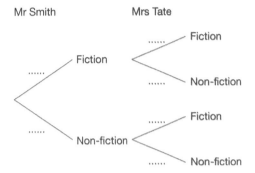

b Calculate the probability that both Mr Smith and Mrs Tate take out a fiction book. **AO2**

c Calculate the probability that only one fiction book is taken out.

7 Zi Ying and Katie go to the canteen for lunch. Main meals are served with either **AO2** mashed potato or jacket potato.

The probability that Zi Ying chooses mashed potato is 0.4.

The probability that Katie chooses mashed potato is 0.7.

Draw a probability tree diagram and use it to calculate the probability that:

a they both choose mashed potato

b they both choose jacket potato

c one chooses mashed potato and the other chooses jacket potato.

Grade 7

8 A pencil case contains 12 pens that look identical but have different coloured ink. **AO2**

Eight pens have blue ink, four have black ink.

Kate takes a pen, then Richard takes a pen.

a What is the probability that they both choose a blue pen?

b What is the probability that they both choose a pen of the same colour?

c What is the probability that they choose one of each colour?

EQ **9** Shamil, Charlotte and Reece are taking their driving tests. **AO2**

The probability that Shamil passes his driving test on the first attempt is 0.5.

The probability that Charlotte passes her driving test on the first attempt is 0.7.

The probability that Reece passes his driving test on the first attempt is 0.4.

Draw a probability tree diagram and use it to calculate the probability that:

a all three will pass the driving test on the first attempt

b all three will fail the driving test on the first attempt

c Charlotte passes the driving test and Shamil and Reece both fail.

d Explain why a tree diagram is the most appropriate diagram to draw for this data.   AO3

10 The probability that Sally is late for work is $\frac{4}{7}$. The probability that Anil is   AO2
late for work is $\frac{1}{5}$. The probability that Richard is late for work is $\frac{1}{2}$.

Draw a probability tree diagram and use it to calculate the probability that on a particular day that:

a all three are late   **b** none of them are late   **c** at least one of them is late.

11 Lucy takes four A-Levels.   AO2

The probability that she will pass mathematics is 0.7.

The probability that she will pass geography is 0.6.

The probability that she will pass biology is 0.85.

The probability she will pass chemistry is 0.95.

Draw a probability tree diagram and use it to calculate the probability that she passes:

a all four subjects   **b** exactly two subjects   **c** at least two subjects.

6.10 Conditional probability

Quick reminder

The term conditional probability is used to describe a situation where the probability of an event is dependent on the outcome of another event.

For two events A and B, the probability of B happening given A has already happened is best visualised using a tree diagram:

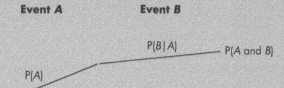

Event A   **Event B**

$P(B|A)$ ———— $P(A$ and $B)$

$P(A)$

Which can be written as: $P(A) \times P(B|A) = P(A$ and $B)$

And then rearranged into: $P(B|A) = \dfrac{P(A \text{ and } B)}{P(A)}$

Grade 9

1 Mrs Harris drives down a country lane on her way to work. The probability that she meets a tractor in the lane is 0.2. If she meets a tractor the probability that she is late for work is 0.6. If she does not meet a tractor the probability that she is late for work is 0.1.

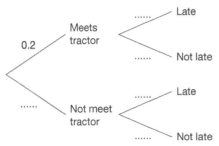

    a Copy and complete the probability tree diagram.

    b What is the probability that Mrs Harris meets a tractor and is late for work?   **AO2**

    c What is the probability that Mrs Harris is not late for work?

2 The head teacher of a school is concerned about the returns of books to the library. He carried out a survey of the students from the lower school, the upper school and the sixth form to see if they returned library books early (E), on time (T) or late (L).

Of the students in the lower school, 26% returned the books early, 70% returned the books on time and the remainder returned them late.

Of the students in the upper school, 10% returned the books early, 58% returned the books on time and the remainder returned them late.

Of the students in the sixth form, 18% returned books early, 80% returned them on time and the remainder returned them late.

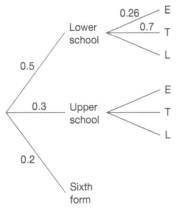

    a Use this information to copy and complete the tree diagram.

    b A student is chosen at random from the school database. Work out the   **AO2** probability that they handed in their library book either early or on time.

    c Another student is chosen at random from the school database. The student is in the upper school. Calculate the probability that the student handed their library book in early or on time.

3 A bag has three green and seven red counters. Two counters are taken   **AO2** at random from the bag, without being replaced.

    a What is the probability that both counters are green?

    b What is the probability that one counter is red and the other counter is green?

4 A tin contains 15 ginger biscuits and 12 lemon biscuits. Florence takes two biscuits at random.   AO2

   a What is the probability that both biscuits are ginger?

   b What is the probability that Florence has a ginger biscuit and a lemon biscuit?

EQ **5** The probability that it will be fine tomorrow is 0.6. If it is fine tomorrow, the probability that it will be fine the day after is 0.85. If it is not fine tomorrow, the probability it is fine the next day is 0.2.   AO2

   What is the probability that it will be:

   a fine both tomorrow and the next day   **b** fine on at least one of the two days?

   Rakesh wants to go cycling either tomorrow or the day after. He wants the weather to be fine.

   c Which day should be go? Explain your answer.

6 A driving school knows from experience that the probability of one of its students passing the driving test at the first attempt is 0.6. If a student fails a test at any attempt, the probability of them passing next time is 0.75   AO2

   What is the probability that a student at this driving school has not yet passed the test after three attempts?

EQ **7** A bag contains six red counters, three blue counters and two yellow counters. Two counters are taken out of the bag at random and without replacement.   AO2

   a What is the probability of taking a blue counter followed by a red counter?

   b What is the probability that both counters are the same colour?

   Calista works out that the probability of picking two different counters is $\frac{18}{55}$.

   c Show that Calista is wrong. What mistake has she made?

8 A test is in two parts: a written test and a practical test. It is known that 85% of those who take the written test pass. When a person passes the written test, the probability they will pass the practical test is 50%. When a person fails the written test, the probability that they will pass the practical test is 12%.   AO2

   What is the probability that someone:

   a passes both tests   **b** fails both tests   **c** passes just one test?

9 A group of pupils take an exam. 25% of pupils solved question 4. Only 5% of pupils solved both question 4 and question 15. What percentage of pupils who solved question 4 also solved question 15?   AO2

10 In a random sample of 50 people it is found that 35 of them like to drink coffee. 20 of these people are female.   AO2

   Calculate the probability that a person who likes coffee is also female.

11 Arwel is going to ride his bike in a race on Monday. The probability that it will rain on Monday is 0.08. If today is the day of the race what is the probability that it is raining?   AO2

12 Kate is a Doctor in a West African hospital where there has been an outbreak of haemorrhagic fever. The probability of coming into contact with a carrier of this disease in the hospital is 0.3. If contact is made with a carrier the probability of contracting the disease is 0.1. What is the probability that Kate has come into contact with a carrier and that she has contracted the disease?   AO2

6.11 Risk

Quick reminder

Risk is the probability of a negative event happening.

$$\text{Risk} = \frac{\text{number of times an even happens}}{\text{total number of trials}}$$

Absolute risk is the chance of an event happening over a period.

For example, 27 people out of 100 will get dementia in their lifetime.

The absolute risk is 27%.

Relative risk is used when you need to compare the chance of an event happening between two groups. Relative risk is the probability of an event occurring in one group compared with the probability of an event occurring in the other group.

$$\text{Relative risk} = \frac{\text{probability of an event occurring in group A}}{\text{probability of the event occurring in group B}}$$

Exercise 6K

Grade 5

1 A motor insurance company insured 500 cars last year. Of these 12 cars were involved in accidents. Calculate the risk that a car will be involved in an accident next year.

Grade 6

2 The risk of dementia for people aged over 65 is $\frac{1}{14}$. In a study of 700 over-65s how many would you expect to get dementia?

3 The risk of getting burnt when sunbathing for an hour wearing factor 10 sunscreen is $\frac{1}{6}$. If 53 people sunbathe for an hour wearing factor 10 sunscreen, how many would you expect to get burnt?

Grade 7

EQ **4** A new pain-reducing analgesic for arthritis sufferers is being trialled. The treatment group took one tablet per day for a week while the control group took a placebo each day.

AO2

	No change	Reduced pain
Treatment	34	345
Control	420	17

a What proportion of people in the control group reported no change in pain levels?

b What proportion of people in the treatment group experienced no change in pain levels?

c Calculate the relative risk of experiencing no change in pain levels in the treatment group compared with the control group.

d Describe what your answer to **c** means.

EQ 5

A study of 156 pupils in a Year 11 cohort studying Maths produced the following results:

AO2

Grade	Attendance		
	>95%	<95%	Total
9–5	95	16	111
4–1	10	35	45
Total	105	51	156

a Calculate the risk of a 4–1 grade for students with <95% attendance.

b Calculate the risk of a 4–1 grade for student with >95% attendance.

c Calculate the relative risk of a 4–1 grade with <95% attendance compared with those with >95% attendance.

d Interpret your results.

7   Index numbers

7.1 Index numbers

Quick reminder

Index numbers compare the price of an item with a base price, usually 100. Costs of goods and services in subsequent years are compared with those in the base year. Then each of these subsequent years is given a number, proportional to the base year, such as 103. An index of 103 means that the prices in that year are 103% of the prices in the base year, or that prices have increased by 3% from the base year.

With chain base index numbers the year immediately preceding the one for which the price index has to be calculated is assumed as the base year. So, for the year 2018 the base year would be 2017, for 2017 it would be 2016 and so on.

$$\text{Weighted index number} = \frac{\Sigma(\text{index number} \times \text{weight})}{\Sigma\,(\text{weight})}$$

Retail price index (RPI) is the official measure of the general level of inflation as reflected in the retail price of a basket of goods and services such as energy, food, fuel, housing and household goods.

Consumer price index (CPI) measures changes in the purchasing-power of a currency and the rate of inflation. The consumer price index expresses the current prices of a basket of goods and services in terms of the prices during the same period in a previous year. This shows the effect of inflation on purchasing power.

Gross domestic product (GDP) measures the total value of all the goods made, and services provided, during a specific period of time.

Exercise 7A

Grade 5

 1   The table shows the annual catch of fish in the Northeast Atlantic by UK trawlers.   **AO2**

Year	1967	1977	1987	1997	2007	2017
Annual catch (1000 tonnes)	1009	922	979	911	886	594

  a Using 1967 as the base year, calculate a catch index for 1977, to 3 significant figures.

  b Using 1967 as the base year, calculate a catch index for 2017, to 3 significant figures.

  c What is the percentage decrease in catch from 1967 to 2017?

  d Using 1967 as the base year, 1963 had a catch index of 111. Calculate the annual catch of fish in 1963.

2 The graph shows the exchange rate for the euro against the pound for each month in one year, 2016.   AO2

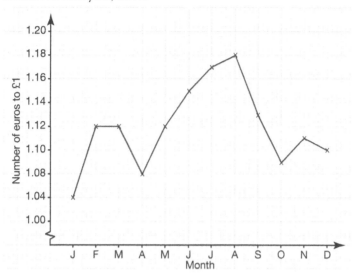

a What was the exchange rate in December 2016?

b Between which two months did the exchange rate rise the most?

c Explain why you could not use the graph to work out the exchange rate of December 2015.   AO3

3 In 2013 the average cost of a bunch of flowers was £2.84. Using 2013 as a base year,   AO2
the price index of the average cost of a bunch of flowers for each of the next five years is shown in the table below.

Year	2013	2014	2015	2016	2017	2018
Index	100	112	132	144	135	142
Price	£2.84					

Copy and complete the table.

4 A manufacturer monitors the costs of a manufacturing process using weighted index numbers.

Type of cost	Weight	Index (2008 = 100)
Raw materials	82	206.5
Labour	185	150.1
Machinery and plant	120	128.6
Administration costs	65	34.8

The price index for each of the components in 2018 is known. The base year for the price index is 2008.

a Calculate the weighted index for the cost of the manufacturing process in 2018. Give your answer to 1 d.p.

b Which type of cost does the manufacturer see as the most important?   AO2

5 The table shows the annual cost of Annabella's car insurance for the past   AO2
three years.

Year	2016	2017	2018
Annual cost	£248	£262	£321

  a Use the chain base method to calculate index numbers for the years 2016 to 2018.
  Give your answers to one decimal place.

  b What do these index numbers tell you about the percentage rise or fall in the cost
  of car insurance from 2016 to 2018?

  c Give a possible reason for the largest of the percentage changes in the cost of
  Annabella's car insurance.

6 The retail price index measures how much the daily cost of living increases or   AO2
decreases.

If 2008 is given a base index number of 100, and 2018 is given 131, what does
this mean?

Grade 7

7 The table below shows information about the retail price index (RPI) and the price   AO2
of broccoli (in pence) in the United Kingdom for August 2018 to March 2019. RPI 2005 = 100.

Year	2005	2015	2016	2017	2018	2019
Cost (pence)	31	46	49	53	67	73
RPI	100	172	173	173	178	199

Describe how the increase in the price of broccoli compares with the RPI over the
10 years to 2015 and over the 12 years to 2019.

8 Steve owns a garage. He wants to find out how the price of unleaded petrol compares   AO2
with the RPI in 2018 and when petrol was at its most expensive per litre in 2012.

Use the table below to calculate these values and comment on the results.

Use 1987 as the base year index = 100.

Year	RPI	Unleaded fuel per litre pence
1987	100	37.9
2009	242	99.3
2010	236	116.9
2011	253	133.3
2012	268	135.4
2013	287	134.1
2014	303	127.5
2015	302	111.1
2016	301	108.8
2017	322	117.6
2018	350	125.2

9 The table shows the chain base index numbers for the price of an annual season AO2
rail ticket from Cardiff central to London Paddington.

Year	2015	2016	2017	2018	2019
Index	114	110	108	105	103

a Describe what the chain base index numbers show about the price of an annual
season rail ticket for the years 2015 to 2019.

b The cost of an annual season rail ticket in 2019 was £11104. Calculate the cost of a
ticket in 2018.

c Calculate whether the cost of a ticket in 2019 has increased by more than 25%
from 2015.

10 The table below shows the average annual price of diesel and the chain based AO2
index from 2013 to 2018.

Year	Diesel price per litre in pence	Chain based index
2013	140.4	
2014	133.4	95
2015		86
2016	110.1	96
2017	120.0	
2018	129.6	108

a What does the index number tell you about the cost of fuel in 2014?

b Complete the table.

7.2 Rates of change

Quick reminder

Crude rates

Crude birth rate is the number of births per 1000 of the population.

Crude death rate is the number of deaths per thousand of the population.

Crude rates are not just limited to birth and deaths but can be employment, cases of a disease etc.

$$\text{Crude rate} = \frac{\text{number occurring in population}}{\text{total population}} \times 1000$$

Standard population

This measure is used to make comparisons between people in different age groups.

$$\text{Standard population} = \frac{\text{number in age group}}{\text{total population}} \times 1000$$

Standardised rate of change

This measure makes meaningful comparisons of age group in different populations or different age
groups in the same population.

$$\text{Standardised rate} = \frac{\text{crude rate}}{1000} \times \text{standard population}$$

Exercise 7B

Grade 5

1 A town with a population of 65 025 has 1560 births in 2017.

Calculate the crude birth rate.

2 The number of adults out of work in a large town containing 250 640 adults is 2134.

Calculate the crude unemployment rate.

Grade 6

3 There were four deaths in a village with a crude death rate of 3.1 per 1000.

Calculate the size of the village.

4 The population of a town is made up of the following age groups:

Age group	Numbers
<20	15 089
20–30	17 065
31–40	25 062
41–50	42 006
51–60	13 620
61–70	15 340
71–80	2 345
>80	1 250

Calculate the standard population of each age group.

5 The number of births in Llanarthne (population 2560) and Llanegwad (population 15 066) was 7 and 28, respectively, in 2018.   **AO2**

Angharad says the birth rate in Llanegwad is higher than Llanarthne.

Is she correct? Explain your answer.

6 The population of a city is shown in the table below.

Age group	Numbers
<20	23 450
20–40	37 087
41–60	123 000
61–80	45 000
>80	12 350

Calculate the standard population of each age group.

7 The population breakdown of a town is shown in the table below.

Age group	Numbers	Deaths
<20	12034	15
20–30	25024	180
31–40	34765	630
41–50	56045	1250
51–60	29876	2570
61–70	19024	3450
71–80	8521	4020
>80	2463	1980

a Calculate the crude death rate of each age group.

b Calculate the standard population of each age group.

c Calculate the standardised death rate of each age group.

d Comment on the standardised death rate.   AO2

8 Probability distributions

8.1 Binomial distributions

Quick reminder

A binomial distribution X is written as:

$X \sim B(n, p)$ ($\sim$ means 'has distribution' B for binomial)

The formula is given as:

$P(X = x) = {}^nC_x \, (1 - p)^{(n-x)} p^x$ **Note: $(1 - p)$ is often written as q**

where:

B = binomial probability
x = total number of 'successes' (pass or fail, heads or tails etc.)
p = probability of a success on an individual trial
n = number of trials.

The mean or expected value $E(x)$ of a binomial distribution is given as $E(x) = np$.

A binomial distribution is a suitable model to use if all four of these conditions are met:

1. The experiment consists of n identical trials.

2. Each trial results in one of the two outcomes, called success and failure.

3. The probability of success, denoted by p, remains the same from trial to trial.

4. The n trials are independent. That is, the outcome of any trial does not affect the outcome of the others.

Note: Use the statistics functions on your calculator to do these calculations.

Exercise 8A

Grade 7

1   Which of the following could be modelled using a binomial distribution?   AO3

    a   The number of packs of cheese and onion crisps in a multipack of 24

    b   The number of 6s when a die is rolled 10 times

    c   The time between failure rates of light bulbs

    d   The number of errors per 100 pages in a book manuscript

2 Which of the following is not a property of a binomial experiment? AO3

    a All trials are identical.

    b Each trial has only two possible outcomes.

    c The probability of success changes from trial to trial.

3 A magazine states that 70% of people who purchase motorbikes are men. If nine motorbike owners are randomly selected, find the probability that exactly six are men.

4 Hospital records show that viral meningitis is fatal in 14% of cases. What is the probability that of ten randomly selected patients, two will not recover?

5 A packet of poppy seeds has a germination rate of 94%. What is the probability that exactly 8 of 10 seeds planted will grow?

Grade 8

6 A manufacturer of valves finds that 16% of valves are rejected because they are too large. What is the probability that a batch of eight pistons will contain: AO2

    a no more than three rejects   **b** at least three rejects?

7 A large supermarket calculates that 3% of eggs from a supplier arrive cracked. A customer buys a box of six eggs. What is the probability that: AO2

    a none of the eggs are cracked

    b at least one of the eggs is cracked

    c exactly two of the eggs are cracked?

(EQ) 8 Electrical components produced by a factory have a 1% failure rate. A customer orders 50 components from the factory.

    a Explain why this data can be modelled using a binomial distribution. AO3

    b Calculate the probability that: AO2

       i none of the components in the order are defective

       ii there is at least one defective product in the order

       iii there are at least two defective products in the order.

    c Estimate the mean number of faulty components per 1000 produced AO2

9 The probability of a call-centre worker making a sale on a customer call is 0.15. AO2

    a Find the probability that:

       i no sales are made in 10 calls

       ii more than 3 sales are made in 20 calls.

    b Estimate the mean number of sales the call-centre worker would expect per 100 calls.

Grade 9

10 A car salesman has a 15% probability of making a sale to any customer who enters his showroom. On average 40 potential customers enter the showroom. What is the minimum number of sales that he will have a 95% certainty of making on any given day? AO2

8.2 Normal distributions

A **normal distribution** is shown as a symmetrical bell-shaped curve.

You use the notation $N(\mu, \sigma^2)$ for a normal distribution.

μ = mean σ^2 = variance σ = standard deviation

To calculate the number of standard deviations that a value is from the mean of a normal distribution you use:

$$\frac{\text{value} - \mu}{\sigma}$$

The 68, 95, 99.7 rule

- Approximately 68% of the data is within 1 standard deviation of the mean.

- Approximately 95% of the data is within 2 standard deviations of the mean.

- Approximately 99.7% of the data is within 3 standard deviations of the mean.

This is illustrated in the diagram below.

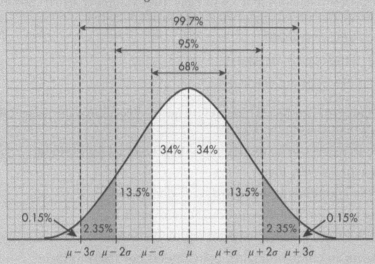

Exercise 8B

Grade 6

EQ 1 Nigel collects the following information in a survey: AO3

gender, height, favourite food, number of cars in the household

Which of these is most likely to be modelled by a normal distribution?

Justify your answer.

2 The amount of time a halogen light bulb lasts is found to be a normal distribution with a mean of 3000 hours and a standard deviation of 500 hours.

What time limits would you expect 95% of the light bulbs to lie between?

3 Kate takes a sample of weights of new-born babies at a hospital. She finds that the weights are normally distributed with a mean weight of 3 kg and a standard deviation of 700 g.

What percentage of the sample would you expect to have a weight of less than 1.4 kg?

4 Cardiff's January high temperatures have a mean of 36 °F with a standard **AO2** deviation of 10 °F, while in July the mean high temperature is 74 °F and the standard deviation is 8 °F.

a In which month is it more unusual to have a day with a high temperature of 55 °F?

The mean high temperature in February in Cardiff is 10 °C with a standard deviation of 2 °C. In August the mean high temperature is 22 °C with a standard deviation of 7 °C.

b Would you be more likely to see a high temperature of 13 °C in February or August?

5 The mean height of adult males in Holland is 181 cm with a standard deviation **AO2** of 7 cm.

What percentage of adult males would you find between 174 cm and 188 cm?

6 The weights of bags of potatoes produced by a farm can be modelled as a normal **AO2** distribution with a mean of 25 kg and standard deviation 0.5 kg.

Calculate an estimate of the probability that a randomly selected bag will weigh:

a less than 24.5 kg   **b** more than 26.5 kg.

7 A variable, X, has a normal distribution with mean 60.

95% of the values of X lie between 45 and 75.

a Sketch a diagram to show this distribution.

b Calculate an estimate of the standard deviation.

EQ **8** The scores for class 11A in a physics exam are normally distributed and shown in the diagram below.

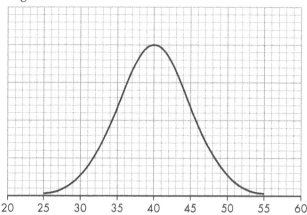

a Estimate the mean and standard deviation.

b The same test was taken by class 11B. The mean score was 44 and the standard **AO2** deviation was 6.1. Compare the results of class 11A with those of 11B.

8.3 Standardised scores

Quick reminder

Standardising a score or value can be used to compare results from different data sets. The standardised score tells you how far the actual score is from the mean. For example, how do you compare your score in a Physics exam to your score in an English exam?

In order to do this, you can standardise both scores using the formula:

$$Z = \frac{X - \mu}{\sigma}$$

Z = standardised score μ = mean

X = score/value to be standardised σ = standard deviation

A positive standardised score is above the mean.

A negative standardised score is below the mean.

Exercise 8C

Grade 7

1. Freya and Daisy compete in a 200 m race. The mean time of the athletes running the race is 27.4 s with a standard deviation of 3 s.

    Freya's time was 28.1 s.

    a   Calculate Freya's standardised score.

    b   Daisy's standardised score was −0.4. Calculate her time for the race.

    c   How could you tell from the standardised scores that Daisy was faster?   **AO2**

2. John's scores in his History and Geography exams along with the mean and   **AO2**
    standard deviation of his classes are shown below.

Subject	John's scores	Class mean	Standard deviation
History	58	61	8
Geography	47	55	10

    Which subject did he perform better in?

3. Harry's teacher told him he had a standardised score of 1.5 in his Mechanics exam. She also told him that the class mean was 72 and the standard deviation 8.

    What was Harry's actual mark?

EQ **4** The mean weight of fish in a fishery lake is 720 g and the standard deviation is 100 g   **AO2**

Rhian catches a fish weighing 620 g

a Calculate a standardised weight of Rhian's fish.

b Rhian's friend Tom also caught a fish. Its standardised weight was 1.3. Who caught the heaviest fish? Explain your answer.

5 The table below shows the scores Becky attained in three Science exams. It also shows the class mean score, standard deviations and the standardised score.

Exam	Score	Class mean	Standard deviation	Standardised score
Biology	63		5	−1.4
Chemistry	80	72	10	
Physics	62	50		0.6

Some of the information in the table is missing. Complete the table.

EQ **6** Stephanie recorded the time she took to travel to work on each of 50 days.   **AO2**

The table shows information about these times:

Time, x (minutes)	Frequency, f
$20 < x \leq 30$	4
$30 < x \leq 38$	9
$38 < x \leq 42$	12
$42 < x \leq 50$	18
$50 < x \leq 60$	7

a Calculate an estimate of the mean time Stephanie took to travel to work.

b Calculate an estimate of the standard deviation of these times.

You may use $\sum fx^2 = 91367$.

Stephanie thinks that the times can be modelled using a normal distribution.

c Is Stephanie correct? Justify your answer.   **AO2**

7 Jada can sell all of the pumpkins grown on his farm to a supermarket, as long as   **AO2**
85% of them weigh between 750 g and 1.5 kg.

Weight, w (g)	$500 \leq w < 750$	$750 \leq w < 1000$	$1000 \leq w < 1250$	$1250 \leq w < 1500$	$1500 \leq w < 1750$
Frequency	22	63	98	53	7

Will the supermarket accept Jada's pumpkins?

8.4 Quality assurance

Quality assurance is used in manufacturing and is the process of checking samples of a product to ensure that they meet the required standards, e.g. a bag of crisps should have a weight of 50 g. Samples are taken at regular intervals and the mean weight calculated. The production warning and action limits are then set:

Upper and lower warning limits are $\mu \pm 2\sigma$

Upper and lower action limits are $\mu \pm 3\sigma$

If the sample mean is above or below the warning limit another sample should be taken. If the sample mean is above or below the action limit the production should be stopped and the machines should be recalibrated.

Samples are plotted on a control chart as shown below.

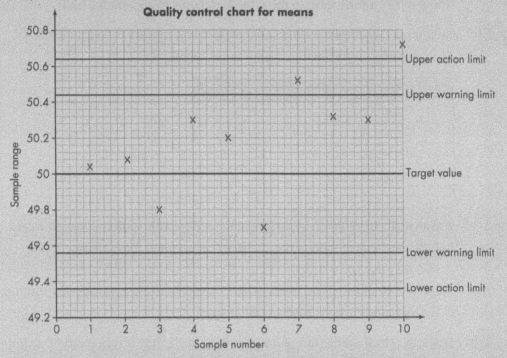

Quality control can also be used for the ranges in a sample. You do not calculate the lower action and warning limits of ranges.

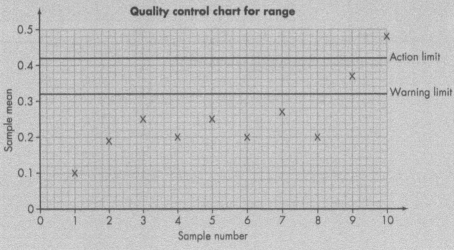

Exercise 8D

Grade 6

 1 A manufacturer makes screws with a mean length of 28 mm and standard deviation of 0.2 mm.

Calculate the warning and action limits for this process.

Grade 7

 2 A manufacturer produces jars of chillies that should have a mean weight of 190 g and a standard deviation of 1.5.

Six samples are taken, and the means of each sample are shown in the table below.

a Plot the sample on a control graph.

Sample	Sample mean in grams
1	190.1
2	192.2
3	191.0
4	193.2
5	190.0
6	191.5

b Calculate the upper and lower warning limits and draw them on your graph.

c Which sample is outside of these limits?

d What action should the manufacturer take?

e What % of jars would be outside the action limits?

3 A drinks machine is designed to fill bottles to 500 ml. Samples of five bottles are taken and the range calculated. The quality control chart shows the ranges for six samples.   **AO2**

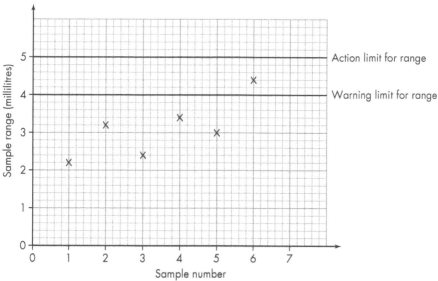

a What action should be taken after the 6th sample?

A seventh sample is taken with values 499.3, 502.1, 504.6.

b Calculate the range.

c Plot the range on the graph.

d What action should now be taken?

4 A machine is programmed to put 19 g of pepper into a container with a standard deviation of 0.02.

As part of quality assurance, a sample of 10 packets is taken every hour and the mean weight calculated.

The results are shown in the following table:

Sample	Sample mean (grams, to 2 d.p)
1	19.08
2	19.05
3	19.03
4	18.99
5	18.94

a Plot the sample means on a suitable control graph.

b Calculate upper and lower warning and action limits and draw these lines on your graph.

c Describe any actions the manufacturer should take.   AO2

5 Chocolate boxes are marked as containing 400 g of chocolates with a standard deviation of 0.5 g.

A sample of six boxes is checked. The mass (in grams) of chocolate in each box is:

402.6, 400.8, 398.7, 403, 402.1, 400.6

a Calculate the mean mass of the six boxes.

b Describe any actions the manufacturer should take, with reasons.   AO2

6 Toothpicks are packed into containers which should contain 150 toothpicks. The standard deviation is 1.5. The range action line is at 3.5.

The results are shown in the table.

Sample no.	Mean	Range
1	152	2
2	148	1
3	152	4
4	152	2
5	150	5

a Copy the graphs below and plot the means and ranges on them. (The mean and range have been drawn.)

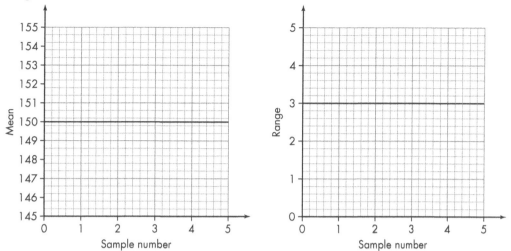

b Draw the warning and action lines on each graph.

c Comment on any issues with the production process.   **AO2**

d What percentage of toothpicks would fall outside the mean action lines?

Answers

ANSWERS TO CHAPTER 1: COLLECTING DATA

Exercise 1A

1. Secondary data

2. Qualitative data

3. Continuous data

4. a Discrete   b Qualitative   c Continuous

    d Quantitative data is data measured numerically, e.g. cost.

5. a Continuous

    b Discrete

    c Discrete (the size of a person's foot is continuous but shoe sizes are discrete).

    d Continuous

6. a Discrete   b Continuous

    c Every item (or person) has an equal chance of being selected.

7. a

Data	Type of data
Species of trees	qualitative
Number of trees	quantitative, discrete
Height of trees	quantitative, continuous
Circumference of tree trunks	quantitative, continuous
Number of branches	quantitative, discrete

    b Height of trees and circumference of tree trunks.

8. Advantages: Collect exactly the data you want, know the data is reliable.

    Disadvantages: Time taken to collect data, may have a limited data source.

9. a He can measure the amount of snowfall that falls this January and then use this information for subsequent years.

    b He can use the data held by local meteorological office for snowfall in that area or region in January for most recent number of years.

    c Quantitative, because it is numerical data.

10. a Qualitative   b Quantitative, discrete

    c Quantitative, discrete   d Qualitative

    e Quantitative, continuous

11. a i. Age   ii. Hobby

    b A census

    c Increased accuracy/reliability

Exercise 1B

1. 458

2. a 36,000   b 70%

3. a 7500

    b She just needs to mark 100 and mix them up so that all the balls have an equal chance of being picked the second time.

4. Dave was closest; the jar contained 200 sweets.

5. a 20000 bees

    b Too much time has passed so the colony could have increased or decreased in this time.

6. a 160

    b Sampling methods identical, populations unchanged, capture has not damaged the fish.

Exercise 1C

1. a Population: All the houses currently for sale in the town.

    Reason: These will give up-to-date information about house prices.

    b Very difficult to make sure he's got information on all the houses for sale at any one time as prices constantly change. It would also be time consuming and expensive.

2. a Any one of: expensive, time consuming, too many people.

    b Population: All the residents of the town.

    Reason: These are the people who would be most affected by the proposed development. Although other people from outside of the town would use the centre, they would be too diverse a group to identify at this stage.

3. Any two from: expensive, time consuming, too much data, difficult to do.

4. A survey

    Any one of: cheaper, less time consuming (quicker), less data to consider, easier to conduct.

5. A survey

    Any one of: cheaper, less time consuming (quicker), less data to consider, easier to conduct.

6. A census

    A survey may not fairly represent those households with children in them. They need to have a clear picture of the age profile in each area.

Exercise 1D

1. a Random sample   b Systematic sample

    c Stratified sample

2. **a** Opportunity sampling

    b Advantage – easy, low cost

    Disadvantage – might not be representative

3. **a** Judgement sampling

    b Advantage – easy, low cost

    Disadvantage – may not be representative of the views of the population

4. **a** 48 32 38 11 02 29 34 03 28 39

    b 48 47 40 11 32 23 07 38 21 11

5. **a** Method 3 is not suitable as surnames are not evenly spread across the alphabet and the method of picking one per letter is not randomised.

    b Method 2 will give the most reliable results as respondents are chosen at random.

6. Total number of children is 60 + 40 + 20 = 120

    From the first group, select $\frac{60}{120} \times 30 = 15$.

    From the second group, select $\frac{40}{120} \times 30 = 10$.

    From the third group, select $\frac{20}{120} \times 30 = 5$.

    Randomly select the stated number of children from each group.

7. **a i** Students at the school.

    ii There may be an unequal proportion of boys and girls asked or there is no evidence of range of year groups.

    iii Take a sample stratified by gender and year group.

    b i People travelling to work in Kevin's town.

    ii Kevin has not considered other methods of travelling to work. His sample only comes from one day of the week.

    iii Take a systematic sample across all commuters by asking people in their workplace rather than during travel.

    c i Whole population

    ii Will only get people who are not at work at that time. Sample is taken solely from one area so is not representative of the population.

    iii Stratified or quota sample

8. Three criticisms of method:

    Only included those people with home phone numbers.

    Small sample size compared to the town's population.

    Only conducted in one evening so excluded all those not at home at that time.

9. **a** There are six strata across each year group and genders.

    b Sample of 50 students:

Year group	Male	Female
1	10	11
2	7	8
3	8	6

   c Random selection: each person is given a number. Then use a random number table or a random number generator on a calculator/computer to select items for the sample.

10. **a** The area of grass within the school playing field.

    b He is only looking at one small part of the playing field and the area he has chosen may be in a sunny or shaded part.

    c Cluster sample (taking samples from across the field).

11. **a** Systematic sampling selects at regular intervals. If the defective corkscrews are produced at regular intervals as well, then this method may give a misleading result.

    b A random sample would provide a fairer picture.

12. From the family group, select $\frac{93}{200} \times 30 = 13.95 = 14$.

    From the couple group, select $\frac{75}{200} \times 30 = 11.25 = 11$.

    From the single person group, select $\frac{32}{200} \times 30 = 4.8 = 5$.

13. **a** The manager chooses a starting point at random and then each male gym user is selected at regular intervals until the number of responses for that day have been collected.

    b This method would be unrepresentative as it excludes all users except male gym users.

    In addition, the sample taken is centred around one day and is clustered around the starting point for the survey.

    c i From the spin class:

    Select $\frac{6}{400} \times 50 = 0.75 = 1$ male, and $\frac{10}{400} \times 50 = 1.25 = 1$ female.

    ii $\frac{24}{400} \times 50 = 3$ female yoga class members.

14. **a** 61.8 million

    b From England, select $\frac{51.8}{61.8} \times 500\,000 = 419\,093.85 = 419\,094$ people.

    From Scotland, select $\frac{5.2}{61.8} \times 500\,000 = 42\,071.15 = 42\,071$ people.

    From Wales, select $\frac{51.8}{61.8} \times 500\,000 = 24\,271.8 = 24\,272$ people.

    From Northern Ireland, select $\frac{51.8}{61.8} \times 500\,000 = 14\,563.1 = 14\,563$ people.

Exercise 1E

1.

No. of children	No. of families
1	
2	
3	
4	
5	
>5	

2.

Result	Tally
Head	
Tail	

3. a It takes a long time to write down the words; it's not easy to see which flavour is most popular.

b

Crisp Flavour	Tally
Plain	
Salt & Vinegar	
Cheese & Onion	
Beef	
Prawn Cocktail	
Other	

4. There is an overlap in categories (£25 appears twice).

Gaps in categories (between £50 & £55 and £100 & £105).

There is no option for other phone makes.

Different models from the same manufacturer have different prices.

5. Reaction time is the dependent variable.

6. A data logging machine attached to a turnstile at the gym entrance would measure how many people entered the gym at specific times. This data could then be analysed to work out when it was busiest. The data would need to be collected over a period of time (e.g. a month) to ensure reliability.

7. Remove units; rewrite in either pence or pounds; discuss how to deal with £150 – remove as it could be £15 or £1.50.

8. Remove units; rewrite in either cm or m.

9. Questionnaire/survey – ask about age (in groups) and how often news is watched on TV.

10. a Primary – survey, a questionnaire (perhaps in a sports shop or gym) to find out features of a magazine that they would find most and least attractive.

Secondary – review other magazines and see what they contain.

b Conduct a survey by selecting a relevant sample from the population of exercise enthusiasts. Use a questionnaire to gain an in-depth understanding of their opinions on lifestyle magazines. Ensure all questions are clear and unbiased and give the relevant information by conducting a pilot study.

11. A spelling test using the same words is given to a group of boys and a group of girls. Using words of increasing difficulty to determine performance. Select the sample of boys and girls at random from a group of similar ages and abilities.

12. a Secondary data – from investigating shop/internet sales.

Primary data – questionnaire/survey.

b Advantages: Secondary data is cheaper and quicker to obtain than primary data.

Disadvantages: It may be out of date; it may be unreliable.

c The data collection sheet needs to accommodate both types of computer and memory capacity.

Memory	Type			
	Desktop	Laptop	Netbook	iPad
0–100 GB				
101–250 GB				
251–500 GB				
501 GB–1 TB				

Exercise 1F

1. This is a leading question, trying to persuade people to agree.

2. a The boxes do not allow for all responses. (There is no box for 'never'.)

b How often do you watch a rugby match during the season?

☐ Never   ☐ Once a week
☐ Once a fortnight   ☐ More than once a week

3. a Question 1: Open question – better to ask a closed question with a range of options.

Question 2: Personal information that respondents may not wish to disclose.

Question 3: Leading question as it presumes enjoyment.

b E.g. How many times have you visited the new leisure centre in the last month? Tick one box.

☐ 0   ☐ 1–2
☐ 3–4   ☐ 5–6
☐ more than 6

4. Advantages (any two from):

interviewer can ensure the question(s) are clear,

interviewer can ensure there are enough answers,

interviewer can ensure enough people are asked (from sample requested), interviewer can ask follow up questions if needed.

Disadvantages (any two from):

can be time consuming,

people may refuse to answer,

interviewer requires expensive training,

interviewer may introduce bias.

5. **a** Beetroot juice

    b Time taken

    c Age of participants; hydration; temperature of environment; time of day etc.

6. **a i** A closed question has a set of answers the respondent chooses from.

    ii People can avoid disclosing their exact age; it groups the data.

    b He could have conducted personal interviews or included self-addressed envelopes.

    c He should have conducted a pilot survey.

    d It assumes the respondent goes shopping and it may have been better to ask as a closed question with a defined set of answers.

7. It ensures that the questions are clear, contain no errors and elicit the required data/answers.

8. **a** A personal interview is more likely to produce responses. There is also the opportunity to clarify queries.

    b May be too time-consuming and expensive to conduct personal interviews.

    c Advantages include:

    easy to collect data,

    anonymous so people more likely to be honest.

    Disadvantages include:

    self-selected sample (you only get the people who are willing to participate),

    you only get people who have access to the internet,

    no way of checking reliability of answers.

9. **a** Without the control group he couldn't be certain that significant weight loss had occurred.

    b Selected pairs should be as similar as possible, in terms of height, weight, age etc.

    c How much participants eat during the trial; whether they were weighed at the same time of day; hydration levels of the subjects.

Exercise 1G

All the given answers cover just one possibility. There are many more.

1. **a** CDs are cheaper on the Internet than the high street.

    b Prices of the same CDs at a selection of different Internet sites and a selection of different high street shops.

    c Ying must make sure she includes all the costs (e.g. postage, travel etc.) and make sure she looks at different categories of CDs, not just the ones she likes.

    d Some CDs may not be available at all the sites/shops. Some prices may be temporarily low because of sales or offers.

    e It might be fairer to compare modal prices rather than means so that extreme prices do not affect the comparison.

2. **a** Young people have better memories than old people.

    b She would have to devise a memory test that she could use to test a person's memory.

    This would have to be given to a random sample of people either stratified by age group or have their exact age recorded as part of the data.

    c She must be aware that some people are better at remembering some things (e.g. objects) than others (e.g. numbers). There is also a difference between visual and aural memory. She must be careful to obtain a range of IQs (i.e. not just young people from her maths set).

    d Older people may not want to give their age or give it inaccurately. Some people may be too busy to take the test.

    e She could use scatter diagrams to look for possible negative correlation between age and memory. If there appears to be a correlation, she could calculate a correlation coefficient to measure it.

3. **a** More boys pass their GCSE Maths than girls.

    b Daniel will have to collect secondary data from the exam boards for a number of years.

    c He may want to consider other grades as well as just passing. He needs to know if the same numbers of each sex take GCSE maths. He also needs to know if the same proportion of each sex take GCSE maths and at what level.

    d Daniel will have to look carefully at how the secondary data is presented (e.g. is it numbers or percentages?). A few years ago there were three levels but now there are just two. Also there was coursework. He will not have access to actual marks.

    e Daniel will calculate averages and measures of spread over the years.

4. **a** *The Sun* uses shorter words than *The Times*.

    b Measure the length of words from a random sample from a copy of each paper on any given day.

    c How big the sample should be? How will he select it – e.g. an article from each on the same topic? He might look at sentence length as well.

    d He may not be able to find two matching articles. He must decide what to do about names, other proper nouns and also numbers.

    e He might calculate averages and measures of spread and draw box plots to compare the results.

5. **a** Boys spend more time playing computer games after school than girls do.

    b Create a survey asking how much time is spent on playing computer games after school and use a random sample of boys and girls selected from the same population (i.e. school year).

c Whether the day the data is collected is important, if age is a factor, the type of computer game.

d Honesty of responses, getting a random sample, getting responses from students of different age groups.

e Show the data on a bar chart, find the mean (or median if extreme data is present).

6. He should carry out a survey, collecting data by asking questions. He needs to decide on the sample he needs to survey, find the best way to collect the data and create suitable questions.

At this stage, it would be best to run a pilot study by asking a small group within his chosen sample. This will allow him to check that the questions are not biased and the results are meaningful, as well as thinking about any other factors that might affect the results.

He can now complete his survey and collate all the results together. He should then calculate the averages (mean, mode and median) and the measures of spread (range, interquartile range and standard deviation). Hamish then needs to determine which results are the most representative and conclude as to whether they provide supporting evidence for his hypothesis.

ANSWERS TO CHAPTER 2: REPRESENTING DATA

Exercise 2A

1. a

Number of pets	Tally	Frequency
1	卌 ||	7
2	卌 卌	10
3	卌 |	6
4	||||	4
5	||	2
6	|	1

b 2 pets

c 77 pets

d 17 students

2. a

Number of brothers	Tally	Frequency
0	卌 |	6
1	卌 卌	10
2	|||	3
3	|	1

b 1 student

c 16 students

3. a

Number of pets	Tally	Frequency
0	卌 ||||	9
1	||||	4
2	卌 ||	7
3	||||	4
4	||	3

b 9 children

c 27 children

Exercise 2B

1. a 66

b 63.6%

c

Number of marks	Frequency
0–3	2
4–7	12
8–11	23
12–15	29

d None of the detail is lost.

e It is easier to work with or easier to read.

2. a

Height (h) in cm	Frequency
$140 \leq h < 150$	4
$150 \leq h < 160$	8
$160 \leq h < 170$	5
$170 \leq h < 180$	3

b 8

c 4

d $170 \leq h < 180$ cm

3. a

Masses (m) in kg	Frequency
$45 \leq m < 50$	3
$50 \leq m < 55$	4
$55 \leq m < 60$	4
$60 \leq m < 65$	5
$65 \leq m < 70$	3
$70 \leq m < 75$	4

b 11

c $55 \leq m < 60$ kg

4.

Pocket money (euros)	Tally	Frequency
5.00–7.99	|||||		6
8.00–10.99	||||| ||||	9
11.00–13.99	||||| ||	7
14.00–16.99	||	2

5. a

Weight w (nearest gram)	Tally	Frequency
$20 \leq w < 25$	||||	4
$25 \leq w < 30$	||||	4
$30 \leq w < 35$	||	2
$35 \leq w < 40$	|||	3
$40 \leq w < 45$	|||||	5
$45 \leq w < 50$			1
$50 \leq w < 55$			1

b 8 books

c $40 \leq w < 45$

d

Weight w (nearest gram)	Tally	Frequency
$20 \leq w < 30$	||||| |||	8
$30 \leq w < 40$	|||||	5
$40 \leq w < 50$	|||||		6

e There is a data point missing as the final range does not include it (52 g). The first table gives a better representation of the original data and patterns are easier to see.

6. a i 19.5 minutes

   ii 24.5 minutes

b To capture the extreme values that lie greater than 50 minutes.

c When the data is not evenly spread across the range, class intervals of varying width are more useful.

d Yes, there is support for her belief as 25 students (81%) completed the homework in less than 35 minutes.

Exercise 2C

1. a 1   **b** 19   **c** 32

   d They had no sausages or toast with their breakfast.

2. a 1

   b 7

   c 6

   d Ginger / auburn

   e 30

   f Mr Khan's group 6.7%; Mr Alam's group 9.4%. The percentage of students with ginger/auburn hair is higher in Mr Alam's group.

3. a 3   **b** 6

   c 15

   d One television and one car: 3 houses out of 30 = 10%; three televisions and three cars: 2 houses out of 30 = 6.7%.

   The number (or percentage) of houses with one car and one television is greater.

4. a

	RS	German	History	Total
Female	35	5	13	53
Male	12	17	18	47
Total	47	22	31	100

   b 18

   c 5

   d 31

   e Hightown: 35%; Newtown 36%. Newtown has a slightly higher percentage.

5. a

	School lunch	Packed lunch	Other	Total
Female	17	9	6	32
Male	21	7	0	28
Total	38	16	6	60

   b 9

   c 0

   d 16

   e $\frac{1}{10}$

6. a

	Male	Female	Total
Watched football	21	24	45
Did not watch football	8	8	16
Total	29	32	61

   b 8

   c 16

   d 72.4%

   e In Alice's survey 75% of the females watched football compared with 72.4% of the males. But she only asked students in two classes; she would need to ask more people in other age groups to reach a valid conclusion.

Exercise 2D

1. a

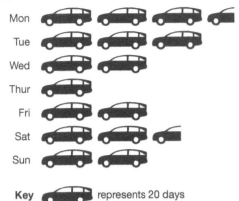

| Mon |
| Tue |
| Wed |
| Thur |
| Fri |
| Sat |
| Sun |

Key represents 20 days

b There would be too many symbols and it would be hard to read off the values.

2. a

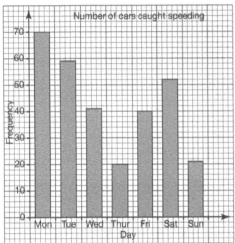

b For example, drivers heard about the speed trap and slowed down.

c Bar chart easier to read accurately.

3. a Carnations

b Roses

c 35

d 30

4. a 17

b

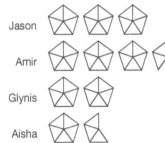

Jason

Amir

Glynis

Aisha

Key  represents 5 texts

c 50 texts

d Glynis sent 10 out of 50 texts = 20%

Exercise 2E

1.

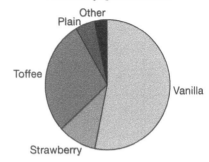

Favourite yoghurt flavours

2. a 45°

b 20 people

3.

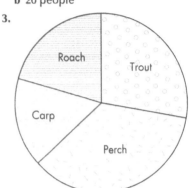

4.

Biscuit	Frequency	Angle
Bourbon	12	60
Oreo	18	90
Hobnob	16	80
Digestive	19	95
Rich Tea	7	35

5. a The proportion of elm trees has been reduced dramatically.

b The pie charts show the proportion of trees in 1955 and 1995. If the total number of trees is the same, then the number of beech trees will have increased. However, as it does not state that these are comparative pie charts, this cannot be assumed. The total number of trees could now be smaller. The pie charts show that the proportion of beech trees is greater, but they do not show that the number of beech trees has increased.

Exercise 2F

1. 23.9 cm

2. Llanarthne pie chart should have a radius of 4 cm.

3. a The number of smokers has decreased, as the area of the 2018 pie chart is smaller.

b 20–24; a decrease

c 667

4. £4551

5. 4 cm

Exercise 2G

1. **a** The y-axis starts at 60, which makes the most popular type (films) look almost twice as popular as cartoons, when in fact there is only a small difference of 15 between them.

    b
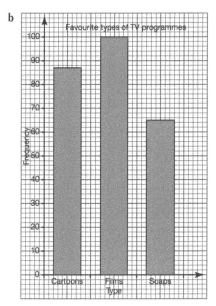

2. There is no vertical scale, so we don't know what the increase in petrol price is.

3. The graph's y-axis starts at 1.0 rather than 0, and the years 2014–2017 have been missed out on the x-axis.

4. **a**
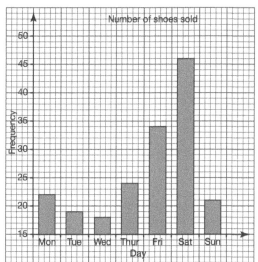

    b The y-axis starts at 15, which makes the busiest day (Saturday) appear to have sold many times more shoes than the quietest day (Wednesday). In reality, Saturday's sales were 2.5 times those on Wednesday.

5. **a**
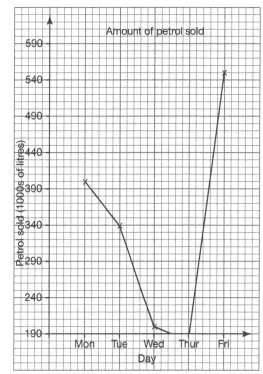

    b By starting the y-axis at 190 000 litres, it makes it appear that no petrol was sold on Thursday.

6. Due to the angle that the pie chart is being viewed from, it looks as though the sector at the front (the 'week after') is much larger than the other two. It is misleading because we cannot clearly judge the proportional size of the three sectors.

7. **a** The second jar looks much bigger than the weight difference suggests.

    b Smaller jar 1.1p/gram compared with larger jar 1.4p/gram. Smaller jar is better value.

Exercise 2H

1. **a**
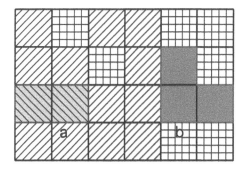

    b See highlighted section **b** on diagram.

    c This area of the reef has lower fish numbers than the rest of the coral reef.

    d See highlighted section **a** on diagram.

    e This area of the reef has higher fish numbers than the rest of the coral reef.

2. a

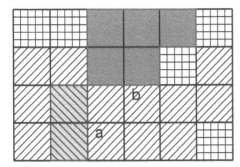

   b See highlighted section **b** on diagram.

   c Without trees in these areas, there will be fewer birds.

   d See highlighted section **a** on diagram.

3. a Aberdeen City and City of Edinburgh.

   b These two cities must have had a lot of people moving to them during this time for work or education.

   c 0%

   d There are many regions shown in the same colour. It would be better to have more shades to differentiate between these areas, e.g. the regions could be split into 0%, 0.1%, 0.2%, 0.3%, etc.

4. a

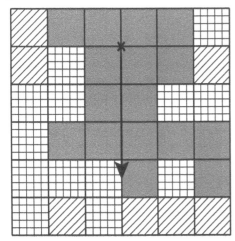

   b See X on diagram.

   c No one is standing near there.

   d See arrow on diagram.

   e Fewer people in this direction.

5. a

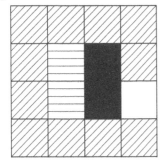

b There are very few nests around the edge of the forest. Most of the nests are near the centre of the forest.

Exercise 2I

1. a

Stem	Leaves
9	7
10	8 5 9 6 8 6 9
11	4 5 3 1 5 3 6 5 1 9
12	3 0 1

Key: 9 | 7 means 9.7 seconds

   b

Stem	Leaves
9	7
10	5 6 6 8 8 9 9
11	1 1 3 3 4 5 5 5 6 9
12	0 1 3

Key: 9 | 7 means 9.7 seconds

   c Range = 2.6 seconds

   d Median = 11.3 seconds

2. a

Stem	Leaves
2	5 6 7 9
3	0 1 3 4 4 5 5 6 6 6 7
4	0 1 1 2 4 6 7 7 8
5	0 2 3 8 9
6	1 2

   b 2 | 5 means 25 grams

   c 25 g

   d 62 g

   e Range = 37 g

   f Median = 40 g

3. a 20 seconds

   b 94 seconds

   c Adults median = 67.5 seconds; 14–16 year olds median = 53 seconds

   d Overall, the 14–16 year olds did the puzzle faster than the adults.

4. a Median = 79 beats per minute

   b Mode = 75 beats per minute

   c Mean = 80 beats per minute

   d The median and mean pulse rates are lower, but the range has increased from 27 to 29, so the patients' pulse rates were lower on average but showed more variation.

   e It shows the distribution of pulse rates clearly and enables the range and median to be found easily. The diagram could be adapted to a back-to-back stem-and-leaf diagram so that the two sets of pulse rates could be compared.

Exercise 2J

1. a, b

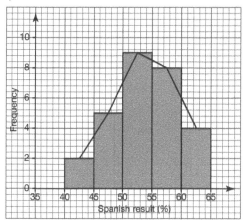

2. a

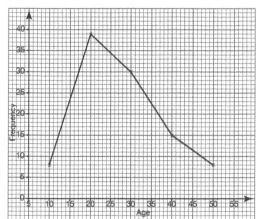

b 77% of the sample are aged below 35 and they would be unlikely to enjoy an article on buying antiques. However, the subject matter of the magazine is unknown and the article might be relevant to the readers so their age might not be a significant factor.

3. That is the middle value of the age group 0 to 10. It would be very unusual for most of them to be exactly in the middle at 5 years old. Also, if you added up the number of other runners, the total is 55 – much more than the 25 in the 0 to 10 group which is the modal class.

4. a

Grade	4	5	6	7	8	9
Frequency	12	16	25	27	15	9
Cumulative Frequency	12	28	53	80	95	104

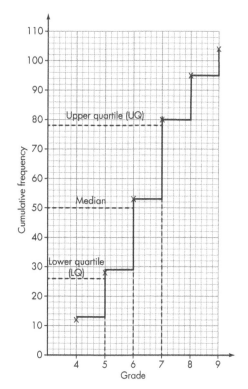

b Median = Grade 6

The interquartile range lies between Grades 5 and 7.

5. a

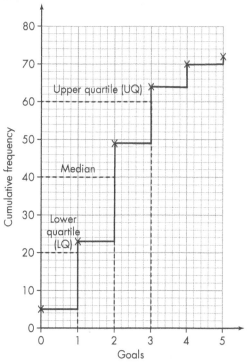

b Median = 2

IQR = 3 − 1 = 2

6. a

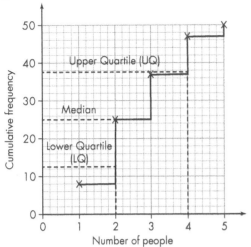

b Median = 2

IQR = 4 − 2 = 2

7. a

Mass, m	Tally	Frequency
$10 \leq m < 12$	Ⅷ III	8
$12 \leq m < 14$	Ⅷ I	6
$14 \leq m < 16$	Ⅷ Ⅷ III	13
$16 \leq m < 18$	Ⅷ Ⅷ	10
$18 \leq m < 20$	Ⅷ	5

b

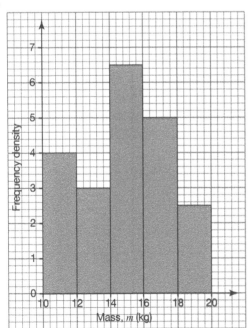

c $14 \leq m < 16$

d $14 \leq m < 16$

8. a

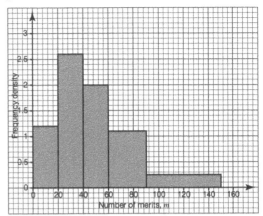

b This year 26 students out of 164 = 15.9%. Last year 32 out of 179 = 17.9%, so a decrease of 2%.

9. a

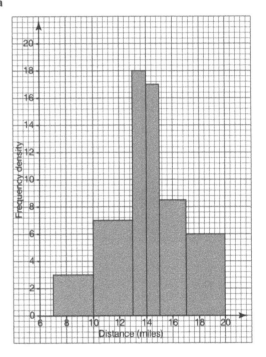

Distance (miles)	7–10	10–13	13–14	14–15	15–17	17–20
Frequency	9	**21**	18	**17**	17	**18**

b 50.5% of cars

c

Distance (km)	3–6	6–9	9–10	10–11	11–13	13–16
Frequency	18	42	36	34	34	36
Frequency density	6	14	36	34	17	12

d

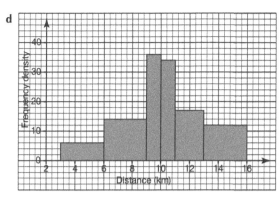

e 50.5% of cars and 26.5% of vans

Exercise 2K

1. Interquartile range = 45–30 = 15%

2. a

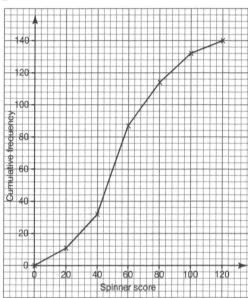

b Median = 54

c Interquartile range = 72 – 42 = 30

d $\frac{17}{140}$

e $\frac{22}{140}$ = 15.7% (1 d.p.)

3. a

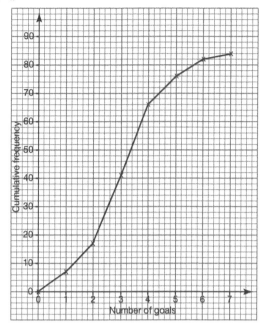

b 3

c 1

4. 11 to 14 seconds

5. a

Time late, t (mins)	Cumulative frequency
$0 \le t \le 2$	23
$2 < t \le 4$	58
$4 < t \le 6$	82
$6 < t \le 8$	94
$8 < t \le 10$	99
$10 < t \le 12$	100

b

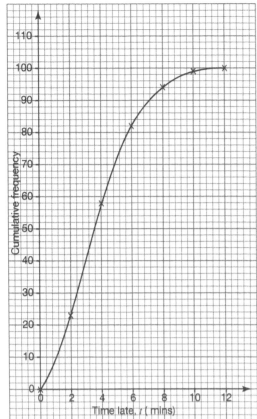

c 3.5 minutes

d No, the bus was more than five minutes late on 26% of the days (or no more than five minutes late on 74% of the days).

Exercise 2L

1. a 30-34

   b India has a higher percentage of younger people and rapid population growth. France has slow population growth.

2. a 0-4

   b 11%

   c USA has slow population growth, compared with rapid growth in Nigeria.

3. a The population is static and will eventually decrease.

   b There are more people above the age of 60.

4. a 8.5%

   b 25–29

   c Slow growth among Europeans and faster growth among Maoris

5. a Kenya rapid growth

   USA slow growth

   Italy no growth, in fact population decreasing

   b Italy 80+

ANSWERS TO CHAPTER 3: SUMMARISING DATA

Exercise 3A

1. 1 goal

2. 3 bedrooms

3. 4, 4, 4, 5, 5, 8

4. 75 g

5. a $12 \leq h < 14$

   b A histogram with equal class widths (i.e. no gaps between the bars) as the data is continuous.

Exercise 3B

1. a Mode = 0 goals

   b Median = 1 goal

2. a 24 tables

   b Mode = £49

   c Median = £47.50

3. The first three must be 4, 4, 6. The other numbers must be bigger than 6, as 6 is the median, but they cannot be either 6 or the same number as each other as the mode is 4.

4. They must add up to £13.

5. a Median of Region A = 6

   b Median of Region B = 7

   c Region B is nearest. It has many more nests and a higher median number of eggs per nest.

6. a Mode = $14\frac{1}{2}$ inches

   b Median = 15 inches

   c Mean = 14.85 inches

   d Either mode as most shirts were this size, or median as it's the middle value best describe the data. Mean is less preferred at its value does not fall into one of the discrete shirt sizes.

Exercise 3C

1. a 28 conkers

   b 30 conkers

   c 6 conkers

2. 91°F

3. a 5.7

   b 58

   c 31

4. 2.15 texts

5. a Mean = 3.5 people

   b Mode = 2 people

   c Median = 3 people

6. 5.8 eggs (to 1 d.p.)

Exercise 3D

1. a

Time taken, x (seconds)	Number of people	Mid-point value	
$20 \leq x < 30$	18	25	450
$30 \leq x < 40$	12	35	420
$40 \leq x < 50$	6	45	270
$50 \leq x < 60$	24	55	1320
		Total	2460

b Estimate of the mean = 41 seconds

c The mid-points of each interval have been used to calculate the mean, not the actual values.

2. a Estimate of the mean = 11.3

b Estimate of the mean = 25

c Estimate of the mean = 14.8

3. a Modal class = $0 < x \leq 20$

b Estimate of the mean = £32.67

4. Estimate of the mean = £122.50

5. a Modal class = $2 < t \leq 4$

b Estimate of the mean = 3.68 hours

6. a Modal class = $8 < t \leq 12$

b Estimate of the mean = 8.8 minutes

7. Estimate of the mean = 207 pages

8. Estimate of the mean = 49.7 marks (to 1 d.p.)

9. Estimate of the mean on Day 1 = 24.25 seconds

Estimate of the mean on Day 2 = 21 seconds

So the estimate of the mean is lower by 3.25 seconds on Day 2.

10. 18

Exercise 3E

In all of these questions, when the best average has to be chosen, alternatives to these answers may be accepted if the reasons support them.

1. a Mode = £8000

b Median = £24750

c Mean = £28200

The two £8000s make the mode too small, and the very large £90000 makes the mean too big, so the median is probably best.

2. The data is qualitative not quantitative, so we can only find the mode.

3. a There is no mode.

b Median = 10 errors

c Mean = 12.8 errors

The median best describes the data. The mean is badly affected by the 45, giving a value bigger than most of the data. There is no mode.

4. a i Mean = 36.05 chocolates

ii Median = 38 chocolates

iii Mode = 40 chocolates

b i The mean will go up, but the median and mode will not change.

ii It looks as if the manufacturer is using the mode, because this represents the most common amount of sweets found in a sample.

5. a Mr Truman's PE class: mean = 32 m, mode = 47 m, median = 31 m

Median, as the 7 could be seen as extreme data and the mode is too high.

b Mr Thom's PE class: mean = 32.9 m, mode = 33 m, median = 33.5 m

Mean, as there is no extreme data.

c Mr Thom's PE class as higher mean and median distance and are more consistent.

Exercise 3F

1. $3 + 36 = 39$

2. Assumed mean of 200

$200 + 41 = 241$

3. Mean, median and mode all increase by the same value

4. Mean = 123

Median = 119

5. £3360

Exercise 3G

1. a 8   b 2.01   c 6

d 4.22   e 6.31   f 8.81

2. a 1.04   b 1.03   c 1.12

d 1.025   e 0.95   f 0.87

3. $1.04^5 = 1.2167 = +21.7\%$

4. $\sqrt[4]{1.04 \times 1.02 \times 1.05 \times 0.97} = 1.01953 = +1.95\%$

5. $+7.88\%$

7. $+24.82\%$

8. $+6.2\%$

9. $\sqrt{0.64 \times y} = 0.72$, $y = \frac{0.72^2}{0.64} = 0.81$; price fell by 19% in the second year.

10. 3, 24, 24

11. Dell = 8.3; HP = 7.8

Felicity should buy the Dell.

12. Kate 7.05; Bethan 7.85; Harriet 5.7

Bethan wins.

13. 1666.67 ml skimmed milk; 1333.33 ml whole milk

Exercise 3H

1. **a** 2.55   **b** 5.74   **c** 4.08

2. **a** Mean = 59.2 marks

   b Standard deviation = 14.8 marks

3. **a** 0.92   **b** 2.14   **c** 6.31

4. **a** Mean = 2.05 pets

   b Variance = 1.40

   c Standard deviation = 1.18

5. **a** Mean = 2.22 televisions

   b Variance = 1.52

   c Standard deviation = 1.22

6. **a** Mean = 7.07 books

   b Variance = 1.03

7. **a** Estimate of the mean = 9.26 kg

   b Estimate of the variance = 14.4

8. **a** Estimate of the standard deviation = 4.43

   b Estimate of the standard deviation = 12.1

   c Estimate of the standard deviation = 6.28

9. Estimate of the standard deviation = 15.9 cm

10. Variance = 7.38

11. **a** Estimate of the mean = 42 minutes

    b Estimate of the standard deviation = 8.06

    c The average difference between the times Stephanie took to travel to work and the mean time was 8.06 minutes.

12. Yes, within this population 88.1% weigh between 750 g and 1.5 kg.

Exercise 3I

1. **a**

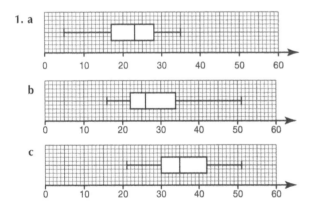

2. **a**

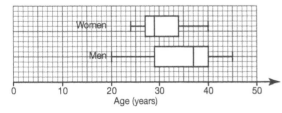

   b The men's median age is bigger, which shows they are older on average. The men's interquartile range is bigger, showing their ages are more spread out than the women's ages. The men's ages are negatively skewed and the women's are positively skewed, showing that most of the men are older than most of the women.

3. **a**

   b White's median price is bigger, which shows the cars there are more expensive on average. Green's interquartile range is bigger, showing that their prices vary more than White's prices. Green's prices are negatively skewed and White's are positively skewed, showing that some of Green's cars are cheaper and that some of White's cars are more expensive, comparatively.

4. **a**

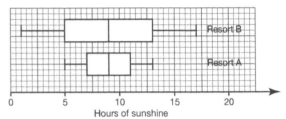

   b Both distributions are symmetrical and have the same median, so the two resorts have the same number of hours sunshine on average. However, Resort B has a bigger interquartile range, so the hours of sunshine there vary more. It has the days with most sunshine, but also the days with least sunshine.

   c Symmetrical / no skew

5. No. There will probably be a few who get very little or even no pocket money, lots who get around the same amount and a few who get a lot of pocket money.

6. **a**

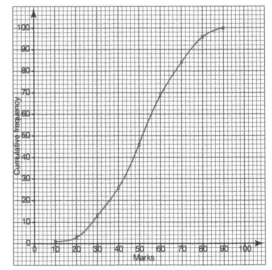

b Median = 52 marks

Upper quartile = 64 marks
Lower quartile = 39 marks

c

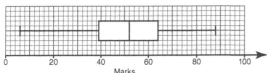

Marks

7. a The top box plot is for Granada, as the mountains would get colder than the beach in September.

b The top box plot has much lower minimum temperatures, a lower LQ, a lower UQ and a much bigger range and interquartile range. Both box plots have the same median and highest temperature.

c Top plot: negative skew

Bottom plot: positive skew

8. a The lightest dog is 5 kg; the lower quartile is 10 kg

b 17 kg

c 13 kg

d 12 dogs. 23 kg is the upper quartile. 25% of the data lies above the upper quartile. 25% of 48 = 12 dogs.

9. a Negative skew; Q3 – Q2 < Q2 – Q1 (100 and 60)

b 150

10. a

Lowest value	22
Lower quartile	28
Median	33
Upper quartile	38
Highest value	55

b LQ – 1.5 × IQR = 13, so no low outliers.

UQ + 1.5 × IQR = 53, so 55 is an outlier.

c

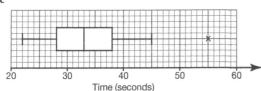

Time (seconds)

11. a A = Q, B = R, C = S, D = P

b P = Symmetrical

Q = Positive skew

R = Negative skew

S = Symmetrical

12. a $\text{Skew} = \dfrac{3(\text{mean} - \text{median})}{\text{standard deviation}} = \dfrac{3(53.2 - 48.7)}{5.6}$

b This is a positive skew. The mean was higher than the median so most of the runners took longer than the median time. There was a greater spread of times above the median than below.

ANSWERS TO CHAPTER 4: SCATTER DIAGRAMS AND CORRELATION

Exercise 4A

1. a

   i Positive correlation – the expected result would be for shoe size to increase as height increases.

   ii No correlation – the expected result would be that no correlation exists.

   iii Positive correlation – the expected result would be ability in maths is related to ability in science.

   iv No correlation – the expected result would be that no correlation exists.

b Variables i and iii

2. a Positive correlation

b Negative correlation

c No correlation

3. Variables a and c

4. a, c

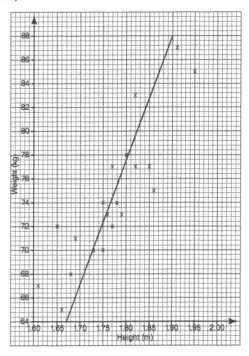

b Mean height 1.77 m; mean weight 74.4 kg

d 67.2 kg

5. a, c

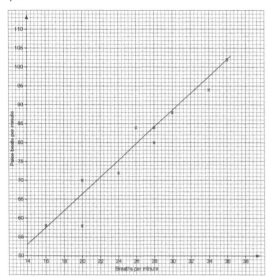

b Mean breaths per minute 26.2; mean pulse beats per minute 80

d 93 pulse beats

6. a Negative correlation

b Elevation increases, temperature decreases

c 1.2 km

d Yes, a change in height above sea level does cause a decrease in air temperature.

Exercise 4B

1. a, b

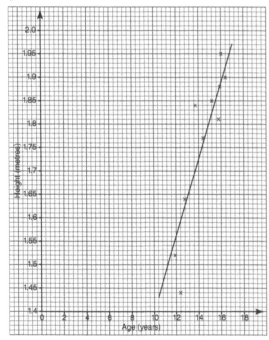

b Mean age 14.45; mean height 1.76 m

c Misca's estimated age = 14.3 years

d People do not keep growing at the same rate once they pass their teenage years.

2. a, b

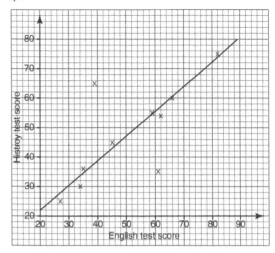

b English mean = 51; history mean = 48

c Jamir. He was a long way from the line of best fit. He should have got around 71 marks.

d Brian. He was a long way from the line of best fit. He should have got around 56 marks.

e 64 marks

3. a, c

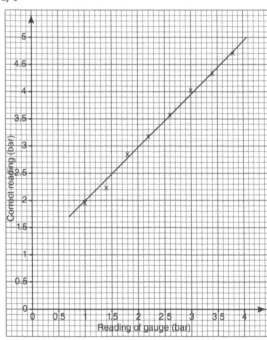

b Reading mean = 2.4 bar; correct reading mean = 3.36 bar (to 3 s.f.)

d $y = 1x + 1$ (exact answer dependent upon line of best fit – allow 10% either side)

e The correct tyre pressure when there is no reading on the gauge.

4. a, c

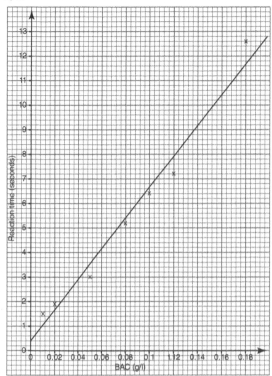

b BAC mean = 0.08 g/l; reaction time mean = 5.4 seconds

d $y = 63x + 0.4$ (exact answer dependent upon line of best fit – allow 10% either side)

e Reaction time = 0.8 seconds when there is no alcohol in the blood.

5. a, c

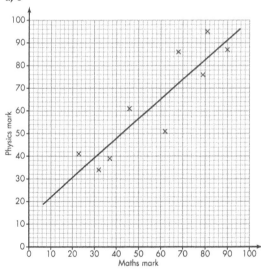

b 57.6, 63.3

d $y = 0.9x + 13$

e You could be extrapolating on very low or high scores.

6. a, c

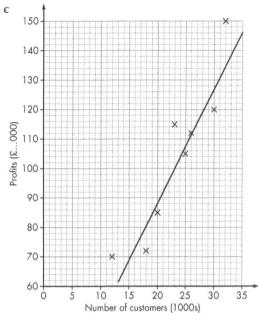

b 23.9, 103.6

d $y = 3.8x + 13.2$

e You could be extrapolating on very low or high scores.

7. a, c

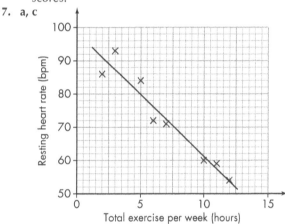

b 7, 72.4

d $y = -3.7x + 98.3$

e A very high heart rate could give negative hours of exercise.

Exercise 4C

1. a Hours of sunshine vs amount of rain: very strong negative correlation (the more hours of sunshine, the less rain).

b Size of diamond vs price of diamond: strong positive correlation (the bigger the diamond, the more it costs).

c Eye colour vs height: weak positive correlation (there may or may not be a relationship between eye colour and height).

Country	Land area (km²)	Population (millions)	Land area rank	Population rank	d	d^2
Austria	83 871	8.21	4	3	1	1
Belgium	30 528	10.42	2	4	–2	4
France	643 427	64.77	8	7	1	1
Germany	357 022	82.28	6	8	–2	4
Luxemburg	2 586	0.49	1	1	0	0
Ireland	70 273	4.62	3	2	1	1
Spain	505 370	46.51	7	5	2	4
UK	243 610	62.35	5	6	–1	1

2. a See above table

 b SRCC = +0.81

 c A Spearman's rank correlation coefficient of +0.81 shows a strong positive correlation and suggests that countries with a larger land area have a large population.

3. a 1
 b 5
 c 4
 d 3
 e 2

4. a

Athlete	5000 m	10 000 m	5000 m rank	10 000 m rank	Difference d	d^2
A	15.36	31.34	5	6	–1	1
B	16.55	32.33	8	7	1	1
C	13.50	30.02	1	4	–3	9
D	14.25	29.44	2	2	0	0
E	17.32	38.23	9	10	–1	1
F	20.12	36.40	10	9	1	1
G	14.48	29.57	3	3	0	0
H	15.45	30.09	6	5	1	1
I	14.58	28.52	4	1	3	9
J	16.04	32.35	7	8	–1	1

 b $\Sigma d^2 = 24$, $n = 10$, SRCC = +0.85

 c +0.85 shows strong positive correlation and suggest that athletes who have fast 5000 m times also have fast 10 000 m times. The reverse is also true.

5. a

Month	Rainfall (mm)	Sunshine (hours)	Rainfall rank	Sunshine rank	Difference d	d^2
January	1.36	1.2	3	12	–9	81
February	1.35	2.7	2	10	–8	64
March	0.75	4.6	1	7	–6	36
April	2.22	5.2	8	4.5	3.5	12.25
May	2.54	5.7	10	3	7	49
June	2.26	7.7	9	1	8	64
July	2.99	5.2	12	4.5	7.5	56.25
August	1.84	5.8	6	2	4	16
September	2.66	4.9	11	6	5	25
October	1.74	3.1	5	8	–3	9
November	1.57	2.9	4	9	–5	25
December	2.09	1.9	7	11	–4	16

b $\Sigma d^2 = 453.5$, $n = 12$, SRCC = −0.59

c −0.59 shows a fairly strong negative correlation and suggests that the more rain there is, the less sunshine there is. The reverse is also true.

6. a SRCC = +0.75

b +0.75 is a fairly strong positive correlation, so the judges mainly agree on who is the best (and worst).

7. Use the SRCC as the relationship is nonlinear.

8. SRCC = +0.63

There is some positive correlation between the marks, so Alicia is probably correct.

9. 7 SRCC = +0.83

There is strong positive correlation, so the longer a person smokes, the worse their lung damage is likely to be.

ANSWERS TO CHAPTER 5: TIME SERIES

Exercise 5A

1. a 08:00   **b** 16°C

    c 16:00 and 20:00   **d** 11.5°C

    e 9 hours

2. a

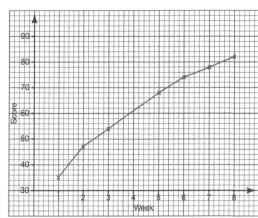

b 61

c The trend is increasing. He is getting better at the questions being asked in the quiz.

d It is unlikely that his scores will keep increasing. His score cannot pass 100.

3. a

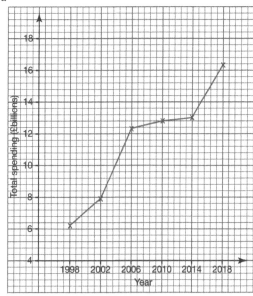

b Estimate of £18–£19 billion.

c The trend is increasing; more money is being spent by tourists in the UK each year. This could be due to people having more money to spend, more tourists, higher prices etc.

d The increase in spending is significantly greater between 2014 and 2018 (compared to the increase between 2010 and 2014).

4. a From 2007 to 2010 there is a slight increase in the number of barn owl eggs hatched.

Then there is a large increase in 2011, and from 2011 to 2014 the numbers increase slowly again. The number stayed the same from 2014 to 2015.

b 12.5 ± 0.5 eggs

c Not reliable; 2021 is too far from the rest of the data.

5. a

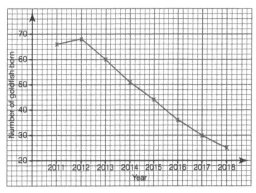

b 20 ± 1 goldfish

c 2013 and 2014

d For example, the pond is getting full up with fish, there is insufficient food, there is a predator living in the pond.

e No, there are too many unknowns in the future for prediction to be possible.

6. a

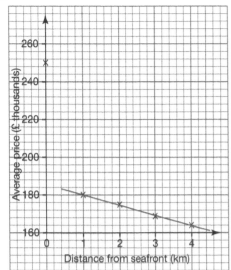

b £159 000 ± 2000

c People want to live near the sea, so the prices are higher as you get nearer the sea.

d No. The prices would not keep going down just because the flat was further away from the seafront.

7. a (134 + 78 + 52 + 120) ÷ 4 = 96

b 106.5, 108.5, 108.75

c

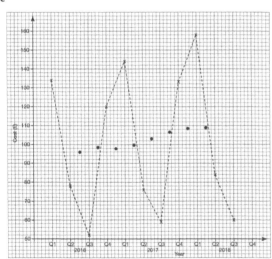

d £22 to £24

e £135 to £140

8. a 4-point moving averages:
42.5, 43, 43.5, 44, 45.

b

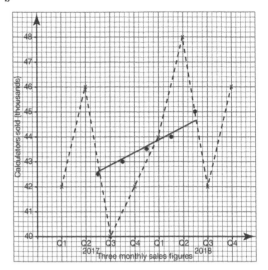

c The trend shows increasing calculator sales with a slight seasonal effect in Q2, probably due to examinations being mostly held in this period.

9. a

Period	Electricity bill (£)	Trendline	Seasonal variation
Jan–Apr	95	94	1.0
May–Aug	63	102.7	−39.7
Sept–Dec	150	107.7	42.3
Jan–Apr	110	110.3	−0.3
May–Aug	71	118.7	−47.7
Sept–Dec	175	122.0	53.0
Jan–Apr	120	123.7	−3.7
May–Aug	76	133.7	−57.7
Sept–Dec	205	138.4	66.6

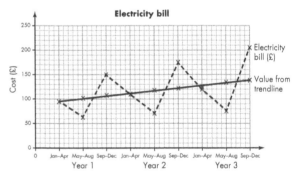

b Seasonal average for May–August =
(−39.7 + −47.7 + −57.7) ÷ 3 = −48.4

10. a £−191.70 (± £3)   **b** £823 (± £3)

c Assumptions: the trend will continue so the quarterly bill will continue to rise linearly; the bill for Quarter 1 will always be higher by approximately the same amount than the value given by the trend line.

11. a

Year	Term	Number of students	3-point moving average
1	Autumn	325	
1	Spring	178	197.3
1	Summer	89	218.7
2	Autumn	389	237.3
2	Spring	234	261.0
2	Summer	160	276.0
3	Autumn	434	287.0
3	Spring	267	300.0
3	Summer	199	

b, c

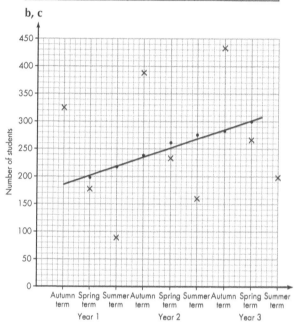

d –122 students

12. a 3226.3

3293.0

3416.7

b 3241

ANSWERS TO CHAPTER 6: PROBABILITY

Exercise 6A

1. a Impossible   **b** Even chance

    c Certain   **d** Likely

    e Unlikely

2. a, b, c

Exercise 6B

1. a $\frac{3}{13}$ **b** $\frac{6}{13}$ **c** 0   **d** $\frac{7}{13}$

2. a $\frac{7}{21} = \frac{1}{3}$ **b** $\frac{10}{21}$ **c** $\frac{17}{21}$

3. a $\frac{1}{52}$ **b** $\frac{1}{4}$ **c** $\frac{1}{2}$ **d** $\frac{4}{52} = \frac{1}{13}$

    e $\frac{48}{52} = \frac{12}{13}$

4. a $\frac{3}{1000}$ **b** $\frac{20}{1000} = \frac{1}{50}$ **c** $\frac{21}{1000}$

    d $\frac{988}{1000} = \frac{247}{250}$

5. $\frac{12}{13}$

6. 0.28

Exercise 6C

1. 5 texts

2. a The outcomes do not have the same probabilities. If the spinner was fair all outcomes would have the same probability.

    b 0.15

    c 60

3. a 180

    b The probabilities of choosing each type of snack add up to 1 because students must choose fish or pizza or pasta or chicken. They can only choose one item.

4. a A ball can only be one colour, e.g. it cannot be both yellow and blue.

    b 42

5. 625

6. 139

Exercise 6D

1. a Equally likely outcomes

    b Historical data

    c Historical data

    d Survey or experiment

2. a $\frac{1}{6}$

    b i 0.08   **ii** 0.09   **iii** 0.106

      iv 0.105   **v** 0.1516   **vi** 0.168

      vii 0.1655

    c 2000

3. a

	Number of times pin dropped	Number of times pin lands point up	Experimental probability
i	100	87	0.87
ii	200	148	0.74
iii	500	335	0.67
iv	1000	584	0.584
v	1500	883	0.5886
vi	2000	1182	0.591
vii	2500	1492	0.5968
viii	3000	1797	0.599

b 0.6 **c** 10 800

4. Wednesday

5. 9990

6. She is wrong because the $P(4) = \frac{1}{4}$ since the '2' occupies half of the spinner.

$\frac{1}{4}$ x 300 is not 100. You would expect less than 100.

As it is an experiment she cannot predict how many '4's she will get.

7. 185 000

8. a The dice looks like it is biased towards a 4, since the relative frequency is much higher than the others and the expected probability of 20.

  b Conduct the test with a greater amount of throws.

9. a $\frac{4}{20} = \frac{1}{5}$

  b Emily has spun the spinner more times so the results should be more reliable.

  c $\frac{27}{120} = 0.225$

10. a Bias **b** No bias **c** Bias

Exercise 6E

1. $\frac{1}{12}$

2. a

		Spinner 1			
		2	4	6	8
Spinner 2	3	5	7	9	11
	5	7	9	11	13
	5	7	9	11	13
	7	9	11	13	15

  b Yes, the probability of getting a total score that is even is 0.

  c The most likely score is 11; $\frac{4}{16} = \frac{1}{4}$

  d $\frac{6}{16} = \frac{3}{8}$

3. a

		Dice 1					
		1	2	3	4	5	6
Dice 2	1	1	2	3	4	5	6
	2	2	4	6	8	10	12
	3	3	6	9	12	15	18
	4	4	8	12	16	20	24
	5	5	10	15	20	25	30
	6	6	12	18	24	30	36

b i 0 **ii** $\frac{4}{36} = \frac{1}{9}$ **iii** $\frac{11}{36}$

c No it is not fair; P(odd number) $= \frac{4}{16} = \frac{1}{4}$ but
P(even number) $= \frac{27}{36} = \frac{3}{4}$.

4. a $\frac{3}{24} = \frac{1}{8}$ **b** $\frac{12}{24} = \frac{1}{2}$ **c** $\frac{6}{24} = \frac{1}{4}$

5. a $\frac{6}{16}$ **b** $\frac{1}{12}$ **c** 0

  d i A six

   ii Probability $= \frac{3}{12} = \frac{1}{4}$

6. $\frac{4}{6} = \frac{2}{3}$

7. $\frac{1}{12}$

8. Probability of one five $= \frac{9}{50} = \frac{18}{100}$. Probability of a total of five $= \frac{1}{25} = \frac{4}{100}$

Probability of a double five $= \frac{1}{100}$. So for 100 people playing, Ishmael would pay out (18 x £1) + (4 x £2) +(1 x £10) = £36. This gives a 64% profit, so he will make money.

Exercise 6F

1. a

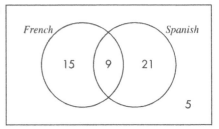

  b 21

2. a 9 **b** 20 **c** 4

3. a

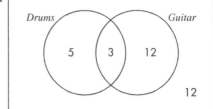

b 3   **c** 12   **d** $\frac{5}{32}$

4. a

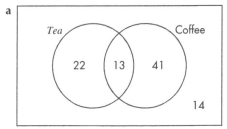

  b $\frac{13}{90}$

5. a Missing 0.2 in rectangle   **b** 0.1   **c** 0.8

6. a $x = 3$ **b** 3   **c** 1   **d** $\frac{17}{80}$

7. a

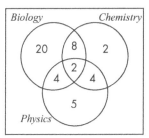

  b $\frac{8}{45}$ **c** 15

Exercise 6G

1. a $\frac{7}{13}$ **b** $\frac{1}{13}$ **c** $\frac{6}{13}$

   d $\frac{12}{13}$ **e** $\frac{6}{13}$

2. a $\frac{5}{12}$ **b** $\frac{4}{12} = \frac{1}{3}$ **c** $\frac{8}{12} = \frac{2}{3}$ **d** 1

   e P(red) + P(blue) + P(green) $= \frac{3}{12} + \frac{4}{12} + \frac{5}{12} = 1$
     = P(red or blue or green)

3. a $\frac{3}{10}$ **b** $\frac{2}{10} = \frac{1}{5}$ **c** $\frac{4}{10} = \frac{2}{5}$

   d $\frac{3}{10}$ **e** $\frac{7}{10}$

4. a $\frac{1}{52}$ **b** $\frac{1}{2}$ **c** $\frac{1}{4}$

   d $\frac{7}{26}$ **e** $\frac{27}{52}$

5. a $\frac{3}{11}$ **b** $\frac{6}{11}$ **c** $\frac{3}{11}$ **d** $\frac{9}{11}$

6. Lucy, whose probability of winning is 0.45.

7. Jack, since his probability is $\frac{2}{5}$.

8.

Type	Probability	Number of questions
Science and nature	0.4	6400
History and geography	0.25	4000
Literature, art and music	0.3	4800
Weird stuff	0.05	800

9. a 0.6   **b** No

10. a 0.8; the probability that a randomly selected person has brown hair or blue eyes

   b 0.2

11. a 0.8   **b** 0.2

Exercise 6H

1. a, c

2. 0.18

3. 0.8

4. a $\frac{3}{64}$ **b** $\frac{15}{256}$

5. a $\frac{1}{169}$ **b** One event does not affect the other.

6. $\frac{27}{125}$

7. a 0.14   **b** 0.3   **c** 0.24

8. a $\frac{25}{676}$ **b** $\frac{441}{676}$ **c** $\frac{105}{676}$

9. a $\frac{3}{125}$ **b** $\frac{9}{250}$ **c** $\frac{27}{125}$

Exercise 6I

1.

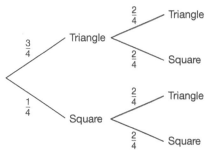

  a $\frac{6}{16} = \frac{3}{8}$ **b** $\frac{8}{16} = \frac{1}{2}$

  c They are mutually exclusive because the outcome cannot be both a triangle and a square.

2. a Red dice   Green dice

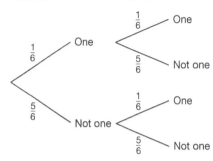

  b $\frac{1}{36}$ **c** $\frac{10}{36}$

3. a Tennis   Darts

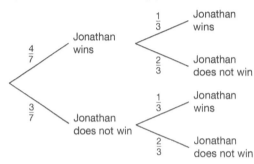

  b $\frac{4}{21}$ **c** $\frac{11}{21}$

4. a Matthew   Daisy

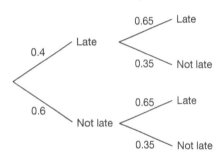

  b 0.26   **c** 0.14   **d** 0.53

5. a Bus   Train

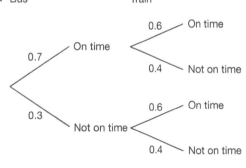

  b 0.42   **c** 0.28   **d** 0.12

6. a Mr Tate   Mrs Smith

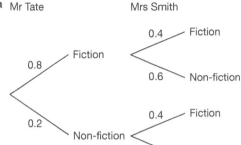

  b 0.32   **c** 0.56

7. a 0.28   **b** 0.18   **c** 0.54

8. a $\frac{14}{33}$ (assumes Kate does not replace her pen, before Richard chooses his)

  b $\frac{17}{33}$

  c $\frac{16}{33}$

9. a 0.14   **b** 0.09   **c** 0.21

  d A tree diagram can show the outcomes of three events and enable the probabilities to be calculated. A sample space diagram can show only two events.

10. a $\frac{2}{35}$ **b** $\frac{6}{35}$ **c** $\frac{29}{35}$

11. a 0.33915   **b** 0.18515   **c** 0.97345

Exercise 6J

1. a

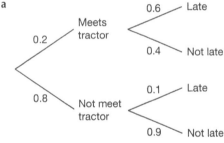

  b 0.12   **c** 0.8

2. a

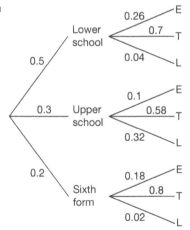

  b 0.88   **c** 0.204

3. a $\frac{6}{90} = \frac{1}{15}$ **b** $\frac{7}{15}$

4. a $\frac{35}{117}$ **b** $\frac{20}{39}$

5. a 0.51 **b** 0.68

c P(fine tomorrow) = 0.6; P(fine day after tomorrow)
= 0.6 × 0.85 + 0.4 × 0.2 = 0.59, so he should go
tomorrow as there is a slightly higher chance of the
weather being fine.

6. 0.025

7. a $\frac{9}{55}$ **b** $\frac{19}{55}$

c The probability that the counters are different
colours = $1 - \frac{19}{55} = \frac{36}{55}$. Calista has only considered
one order in which the counters can be selected,
so her probability is half the value it should be.

8. a 0.425 **b** 0.132 **c** 0.443

9. 20%

10. $\frac{4}{7}$

11. 0.56

12. 0.03

Exercise 6K

1. 0.024

2. 50

3. 8.8 so 9 people

4. a $\frac{420}{437}$ **b** $\frac{34}{379}$ **c** 0.09

d The treatment group had 0.09 times more chance
of experiencing no change in pain levels than the
control group, which suggests that the painkiller is
effective.

5. a 0.686 **b** 0.095 **c** 7.2

d The risk of a grade 4–1 for students with <95%
attendance is 7.2 times greater than for those with
>95% attendance.

ANSWERS TO CHAPTER 7: INDEX NUMBERS

Exercise 7A

1. a 91.4 **b** 58.9

c 41.1% reduction

d 1 119 990 tonnes

2. a £1 = €1.10

b January and February

c There is no trend in the data.

3.

Year	2005	2006	2007	2008	2009	2010
Index	100	112	132	144	135	142
Price	£2.84	£3.18	£3.75	£4.09	£3.83	4.03

4. a Weighted index = 138.0 **b** Labour

5. a 2016–2017 = 105.6
2017–2018 = 122.5

b From 2016 to 2017 her car insurance rose by 5.6%,
whilst from 2017 to 2018 her car insurance rose by
22.5%.

c Answers might include: She bought a new car,
added other people to her insurance; had a crash
or received points on her driving licence.

6. General cost of living in 2010 rose 31% compared with
2000.

7. $\frac{46}{31} \times 100 = 148$ below RPI

$\frac{73}{31} \times 100 = 235$ above RPI

8. 2012
$\frac{135.4}{37.9} \times 100 = 357.3$ the increase in price was above
RPI of 268.

2018
$\frac{125.2}{37.9} \times 100 = 330.3$ the increase in price was below
RPI of 350.

9. a Increased each year by a decreasing percentage

b £10 780.58

c 1.1 × 1.08 × 1.05 × 1.03 = 1.28
28% increase

10. a Price has dropped.

b

Year	Diesel price per litre (in pence)	Chain base index
2013	140.4	
2014	133.4	95
2015	114.8	86
2016	110.1	96
2017	120.0	109
2018	129.6	108

Exercise 7B

1. 24 births per 1000

2. 8.5 per 1000 adults

3. 1290

4.

Age group	Numbers	Standard population
<20	15089	114.5
20–30	17065	129.5
31–40	25062	190.2
41–50	42006	318.8
51–60	13620	103.4
61–70	15340	116.4
71–80	2345	17.8
>80	1250	9.5
Total	131777	

5. Llanathne birth rate = 2.73 per 1000

Llanegwad birth rate = 1.86 per 1000

Angharad is wrong

6.

Age group	Numbers	Standard population
<20	23450	97.3
20–40	37087	154.0
41–60	123000	510.6
61–80	45000	186.8
>80	12350	51.3
Total	240887	

7. a, b, c

Age group	Numbers	Deaths	Crude rate	Standard population	Standardised rate
<20	12034	15	0.080	64.1	0.005
20–30	25024	180	0.959	133.3	0.128
31–40	34765	630	3.355	185.2	0.621
41–50	56045	1250	6.658	298.5	1.987
51–60	29876	2570	13.688	159.1	2.178
61–70	19024	3450	18.375	101.3	1.862
71–80	8521	4020	21.411	45.4	0.972
>80	2463	1980	10.546	13.1	0.138
Total	187752				

d The 51–60 age group has the highest rate.

The <20 age group has the lowest rate.

ANSWERS TO CHAPTER 8: PROBABILITY DISTRIBUTIONS

Exercise 8A

1. a, b

2. c

3. 0.267

4. 0.264

5. 0.099

6. a 0.973   **b** 0.123

7. a 0.833   **b** 0.167

   c 0.012

8. a There are only two possible outcomes; P(failure) = 1 – P(success).

   b i 0.605   **ii** 0.395   **iii** 0.089

   c 10

9. a i 0.197   **ii** 0.3523

   b 15

10. ≤ 2 is 5% so 3 or more for 95%

Exercise 8B

1. Height – continuous data

2. 95% of data is found between + and – 2 standard deviations

3000 – (2 × 500) = 2000 hours

3000 + (2 × 500) = 4000 hours

3. 2.5%, i.e. 2 standard deviations

4. a July = 2.4sd

   January = 1.9sd

   More unusual in July.

   b February = 1.5sd

   August = 1.29sd

   More likely in August.

5. 68%

6. a 16%   **b** 0.15%

7. a

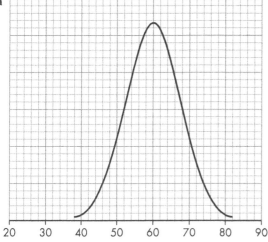

b $(75 - 45) \div 4 = 7.5$

8. a Mean is 40 (centre value)

SD is approximately $(55 - 25) \div 6 = 5$ (99.7% of values)

b The mean mark was higher so the students in 11B scored higher on average; the standard deviation was higher so the average difference between the students' scores and the mean was greater.

Exercise 8C

1. a $\frac{7}{30}$ **b** 26.2s

c Daisy's standardised score is negative so it was less than the mean, while Freya's standardised score was positive so it was greater than the mean.

2. History standardised score = −0.375

Geography standardised score = −0.8

John did better in History because the standardised score is closer to zero.

3. 84

4. a −1

b Tom (a positive standardised score so it is above the mean)

5.

Exam	Score	Class mean	Standard deviation	Standardised score
Biology	63	70	5	−1.4
Chemistry	80	72	10	0.8
Physics	62	50	20	0.6

6. a 41.98 = 42.0 minutes (3 s.f.)   **b** 8.06 minutes

c 3 × standard deviation = 3 × 8.06 = 24.19 minutes. 41.98 − 24.19 = 17.79 minutes; 41.98 + 24.19 = 66.17 minutes.

100% of the times lie within 3 standard deviations of the mean, so the times can be modelled using a normal distribution.

7. Percentage between 750g and 1.5kg = $\frac{214}{243} \times 100$ = 88% so yes, the supermarket will accept Jada's pumpkins.

Exercise 8D

1. Lower warning limit: 27.6; upper warning limit: 28.4

Lower action limit: 27.4; upper action limit: 28.6

2. a

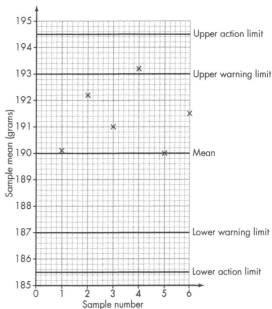

b 187 and 193

c Sample 4

d Take another sample

e 100 − 99.7 = 0.3%

3. a Take another sample

b 5.3

c Correctly plotted point

d Machine is reset

4. a

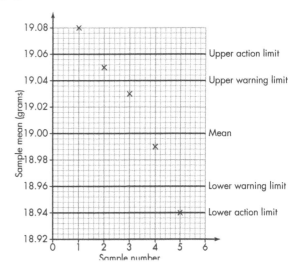

b Lower warning limit: 18.96; upper warning limit: 19.04

Lower action limit: 18.94; upper action limit: 19.06

c Another sample taken after samples 2 and 5. Reset machine after sample 1.

5. **a** 401.3

   b The manufacturer should take another sample as 401.3 is outside the warning limit of 401.

6. **a** Points plotted

   b Action warning lines drawn

   Range line at 3.5

   Mean lines: Warning 147–153,
   Action 145.5–154.5

   c Means fall within warning limits. The ranges on samples 3 and 5 are above the action line, so the process should be stopped and the machines should be checked.

   d 0.3%